The

Borrowing Money

Guide©

A "How-To" Book for Consumers

Written by: Joseph R. Miller

Edited by: Julie Miller

Cover Design and Layout by: Julie Miller

JLM Publishing wishes to specially thank the following reviewers for their time and contribution:

- Charles Mark Hall: Senior Underwriter, 16 years in banking.
- Paula P. Johnson: Senior Underwriter, Branch Lender, 18 years in banking.
- William A. Miller: Licensed N.J. Real Estate Agent, 25 years.
- Carol Rudolph: Mortgage Loan Officer, 6 years in mortgage lending.
- David H. Lepard, Ph.D.: Author and creator of the Professional Enhancement Program.

Published by:
JLM Publishing
Winston-Salem, N.C.

Printed by:
Jostens
Winston-Salem, N.C.

Library of congress catalog card no: TBD

International Standard Book No. 0-9729855-0-6

Printed in the United States of America

This book is dedicated to my wife, Julie,
for her love, support, and encouragement.

Preface

A small investment of time reading this book can save you hundreds of dollars in closing costs and/or thousands of dollars in finance charges (interest) by helping you to properly borrow money. The purpose of this book is to give you *unbiased* information about borrowing money and an *understanding* of the processes involved, which will help you to get the right loan for your *individual* credit situation. This book will also help you avoid costly credit mistakes and show you how to *protect* one of your most prized assets, your credit. This easy-to-read reference guide was written as a resource tool that you can refer to *throughout* your borrowing life. The Borrowing Money Guide© will also prove very useful for *teaching* young people about the importance of building good credit, educating them on how to borrow money, and helping them to become responsible consumers.

Banks, credit unions, finance companies and other financial lending institutions offer many different loan products. These loan products are accompanied with solicitation pitches given by loan officers or commissioned lenders to promote or sell certain products. All of these lending institutions are in the business of profiting off of your need to borrow their product…money! Consumers should think of getting a loan in the same way they do when buying a product. **As a consumer, it is up to you to seek out the best deal at the best price.** The Borrowing Money Guide© will make sure that you get the *best* loan price and the *best* kind of loan by teaching you what different loan products are available, how to confidently discuss loan terms and credit, and what questions to ask loan officers or commissioned lenders who are trying to sell you this product at a profit.

The Borrowing Money Guide© is written for the everyday consumer. Each section is designed to address a particular borrowing need or a certain credit situation. What that means is that the sections can be read on an "as needed" basis. Each section is arranged by chapters that explain (using simple terms) the steps involved in order for you to get the right loan that *best* fits your current financial need or credit situation.

Sections One through Four discuss the four main types of consumer loans. **Section One is titled "The First Time Home Buyer"**. This section coaches people on how to prepare to apply for a mortgage loan, how to qualify for the loan, and the steps involved in order to close the loan. **Section Two is titled "Refinancing Your Mortgage Loan"**. This section educates readers about when to refinance, how to prepare and qualify for a loan, and what different types of mortgage loans are available. **Section Three is titled "The Home Equity Loan"** and is for people who are interested in getting a second mortgage loan. This section clearly shows what type of a second mortgage loan they will need, how they can find the right loan to meet their particular need, and how to get prepared to apply for and qualify for the loan. **Section Four is simply titled "The Consumer Loan"**. This section defines and compares the three main types of consumer loans, describes what type of loan is best for certain situations, and demonstrates how to prepare and qualify for the loan. Examples are provided to illustrate the points.

Sections Five and Six discuss unique credit situations. **Section Five is titled "The Five Most Common Credit Issues"**. This section instructs readers on how to establish credit, when to cosign or not on a loan, what to do in case of a divorce (and how it might affect a credit rating), how to re-establish credit, and how to overcome the credit effects of filing a bankruptcy. **Section Six is simply titled "Fraud"**. This section reveals the two main types of credit fraud, provides tools to use in the event that you become a victim of identify theft, and lessens your chances of becoming a victim of credit fraud by pointing out potential fraud opportunities.

The Borrowing Money Guide⊚ is *a great resource tool* that is to be used throughout your "borrowing money" life! It covers all the scenarios that a typical consumer may encounter. For updated information, other links of interest, or to order additional books please visit our website www.theborrowingmoneyguide.com.

Table of Contents

SECTION V THE FIVE MOST COMMON CREDIT ISSUES

SECTION VI FRAUD

SECTION VII GLOSSARY

Legend:

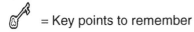 = Key points to remember

= Recommended ideas to consider

Section I
The First Time Home Buyer

Introduction

The first time home buyer guide is specifically written for the inexperienced borrower who is attempting to buy his or her first home. It is designed to make people more comfortable with getting a mortgage loan by explaining and simplifying the loan process. This section will help you to prepare for the mortgage loan, to make sure that you are buying a house that you can afford, and to show you how to qualify for the loan. The first thing that you need to do is to decide that you want to buy a house. Having made that decision, the loan process has just started.

Chapter 1: Getting Your Financial Affairs in Order

Once you have decided to buy a house, the next thing that you need to do is to get your financial affairs in order. **From the time that you apply for the mortgage loan, it is important that you do not make any major purchases either on credit or with cash until** *after* **you close your loan** because these purchases could affect closing. After borrowers have been pre-approved for a mortgage loan, they may be tempted to start spending money or buying new furniture and appliances for the new house on credit. This is a mistake for two reasons. The first reason is that there are generally additional costs that will arise from either the loan closing, the moving process, or from unexpected minor repairs to the house. The second reason is that it usually takes forty-five to sixty days until the mortgage loan is actually closed and the paperwork is signed. The mortgage company can (and sometimes will) reorder your credit report right before final approval is granted. If any new debts show up in your credit file, or there are recent credit inquiries that need to be investigated, your loan could be delayed. In addition, if any new debt is incurred, then your debt-to-income ratio, which has to do with how much you make and how much you owe, will have to be recalculated. This situation could potentially cause your loan to fall outside of the bank's lending guidelines and you could be turned down for the loan. (The debt-to-income ratio is discussed further in Chapter Two.)

If you think you have established good credit and pay your bills on time, then you might be tempted to skip ahead to the next chapter. But don't fool yourself, you might have some credit blemishes or some "slow pay" history in your credit file that you may not know is there. Also, it is possible that some company could have erroneously reported delinquencies to your credit file. For these reasons, it is advisable that you continue reading. These credit blemishes or "slow pay" histories will be uncovered by the mortgage loan officer or underwriter and will slow the application process or cause your loan to be declined.

If you have not reviewed your credit report in over a year it is advisable to review it now. You can request a copy of your credit file by contacting one of the three major credit bureau reporting agencies (Equifax, Experian or TransUnion) listed at the end of Section Six, Chapter Four. The credit report should cost you less than fifteen dollars, but it is well worth it. A few states have a law that allows you to request and review a copy of your credit file free of charge at least once a year.

When you receive your credit file, check the report closely for any discrepancies or errors. If there are any errors or disputed delinquencies, you will be able to dispute those references and accounts through the credit bureau agency where you ordered the report. Along with the credit report package will be a form and information on how to go about disputing any data contained in the report. Another way to dispute the credit reference is to contact the creditor directly. **If you have contacted the creditor directly and a representative has agreed to correct the error, make sure that you get the correction *in writing*.** I have seen many situations in which a borrower will state on a loan application that a collection has been paid off or that a late payment error has been corrected, but comes to find out that the creditor has not reported the correct information to any credit bureau. Other times, the information might only get reported to one of the credit bureau agencies, but not the primary one being used for your loan. This could either cause a delay in the verification process, cause the loan to be declined, or cause the credit reference to remain against you. Having the credit reference remaining to count against you could result in a lower credit grade for you and potentially force you to pay a higher interest rate. **As a rule, you should keep any correspondence, including written corrected account information, for at least the next five to seven years.**

If you have any current delinquencies, you need to pay them. **The better your credit is, the better rate you will get, and the less money you will need for the down payment.** The reason for this is that the higher your credit score is, based on statistical models, the less likely it will be that you default or become late with your mortgage payment. Therefore, your mortgage loan will cost less to service and the savings are passed on to you in the form of a lower interest rate. Typically, anyone with a credit score in the range of 620 to 650 or higher, with reasonably good overall credit, who does not have a bankruptcy on record within the last seven years, and does not have any unpaid judgments or collections against them will be able to get the preferred mortgage interest rates.

If you have filed a bankruptcy in the last ten years, you should get your bankruptcy paperwork together, including the discharge papers. You might not need them if your bankruptcy was discharged over five years ago, but it is best to be prepared so that if they are required, the loan process will not be delayed. Another reason you may need your bankruptcy discharge paperwork is that perhaps not all of the credit that was included in the bankruptcy was reported properly. Some creditors might continue to show an account as delinquent, indicating that you still owe them money, or as if they charged off your account when, in fact, it was discharged in the bankruptcy and you are no longer responsible for that particular debt. By having your bankruptcy discharge paperwork readily available, you will be able to prove what debts were actually a part of the bankruptcy filing. In addition, be prepared to discuss and provide a written explanation as to why you filed a bankruptcy or why you have had any late payments.

A good prerequisite to becoming a homeowner is being a renter. Establishing a record of being able to pay your rent on time indicates to the lender that you will probably pay your mortgage on time. In addition, being able to budget your money in order to pay your utility bills on time will show your ability to pay them on time in your new house. If you pay rent to an apartment complex or company, you should be able to get a signed six or twelve-month rent verification letter. If you pay rent to a private individual, you will need to gather your last six to twelve months of cancelled rent checks or bank statements to prove that you have paid your rent on time. Also, bring along a copy of the signed lease agreement.

Obtaining a mortgage loan and buying a house is not only reserved for married couples in today's borrowing money environment. Becoming a homeowner can happen for whomever is able to qualify for a mortgage loan. There are many different types of family groups, couples, and living arrangements in today's society. **When people apply jointly for a mortgage loan, everyone involved needs to realize that the mortgage contract will be a long-term commitment.** Most mortgages are for fifteen to thirty years. If the relationship with the co-borrower does not work out, you cannot just walk away from the house and mortgage loan obligation as simply as you can if you were a renter.

To summarize how to get your financial affairs in order:

- Order a copy of your credit file from one of the three main credit reporting agencies.
- Ensure that all of the information being reported is accurate. Make corrections if needed and get it in writing.
- If you have any current delinquencies, you need to pay them.
- If you filed a bankruptcy within the last ten years, then have your bankruptcy discharge papers available.
- If you currently rent, obtain a signed rent verification letter from your landlord and have available at least the last six months of bank statements or cancelled rent checks.

Chapter 2: The Down Payment

Getting money together for the down payment is a lot easier than it was twenty or thirty years ago. In most cases, you do not need to put down twenty percent of the purchase price for the cash down payment as required in the past. Lenders are a lot more flexible with regard to the down payment and there are a variety of ways to obtain it. For people with a very good credit score and a good debt-to-income ratio, there are now mortgage loans available that require as little as one to three percent cash down. Some special programs even offer zero percent down payment for qualified buyers. Your mortgage loan officer (the contact person from the mortgage company you choose) will let you know for which program(s) you qualify. Those low down payments are great if you qualify, but the majority of first time home buyers will need at least three to five percent of the purchase price of the home for the down payment and closing costs. If you are getting a conventional mortgage loan, and you do not have twenty-percent cash as a down payment, then an extra monthly payment (called PMI or Private Mortgage Insurance) will be added to your escrow account. This can be a substantial monthly payment in and of itself. "PMI" will be explained in more detail in Chapter Four and "escrow" in Chapter Five.

For their down payment, most first time home buyers will either use money from their current checking or savings account, from an investment or brokerage account, get money from a parent or a close relative, or take it from their retirement/401K account. To verify that you have the cash on hand for the down payment, you will need to provide the lender with your last two monthly bank statements. If you are getting the money from a family member, then have this person write a statement that the money is a "gift" and does not have to be repaid. Another good idea, to help lessen the percentage of your down payment, is to have your real estate agent negotiate to have the seller of the property pay some of the closing costs. Sometimes the seller is anxious to sell his or her property and will agree to credit you back some of the closing cost. You will not actually receive any cash, but the credit will show up on the settlement statement when you close the loan.

Another option for obtaining the down payment money is to borrow from, or make an early withdrawal with *no penalty* from, the 401K or retirement account through your employer as a first time home buyer. If you can borrow against your retirement account, make sure that you will be able to afford this new monthly payment along with your new mortgage payment. Before you do this, check with the human resource department where you work and with your tax advisor to make sure that there is no substantial tax penalty for withdrawing the money as a first time home buyer. If you have to pay a large penalty or have to forfeit a substantial part of your retirement fund to pay taxes, then it might not be beneficial to withdraw the down payment money from your retirement account. **The key is to get the down payment money into your checking or savings account as soon as you have the cash together so that it can be verified.** So remember, get this money into your account as soon as possible!

The Debt-to-Income Ratio

Another way for you to obtain the necessary down payment money is to get a cash advance on a credit card. However, you will need to make sure that the new monthly payment for this credit card advance would not affect your debt-to-income ratio substantially. **Your debt-to-income ratio should remain less than forty percent in order to qualify for the best interest rates offered.** Most mortgage companies' debt-to-income ratio underwriting guidelines fall between thirty-six and forty percent. However, there are loan programs and companies that lend money to people with higher debt-to-income ratios (up to fifty percent, or on a rare occasion, to sixty percent). But these loan programs will typically charge a higher interest rate and will generally cost more in terms of closing costs, fees, and down payment money.

The purpose of the debt-to-income ratio is to determine if you can afford to repay your debts in the eyes of the credit grantor. It is calculated by adding together your total monthly debts or loans (not including utility bills) that you owe, adding in the proposed new monthly mortgage payment (that will be discussed in Chapter Four), then divide that number by your gross monthly income. Your gross monthly income is the amount of money you earn before any taxes, insurance, or other deductions are taken out.

Example:

Do not include	Current Rent	$3,000	Your Income
Do not include	Cell Phone	+2,000	Spouses Income
Do not include	Auto Ins.	$5,000	Total Family Income
$50.00	Credit Cards		
+325.00	Car Loans	$1,750	Total Debts
+75.00	Student Loan	÷5,000	Family Income
+1,300.00	New Mortgage	**35%**	**Debt-to-Income Ratio**
$1,750.00	Total Monthly Debts		

As you can see in this example, you do not include your current rent payment, if you have one, because you will be moving into your new residence that will have a mortgage payment. Also, you will notice that you do not include any utility bills (such as electric bill, insurance bill, cable bill, or phone bill). For your charge cards or lines of credit, a good rule of thumb is to use three percent of your current balance as a monthly payment when figuring your debt-to-income ratio. For your personal or installment loans, you will use the regular monthly payment. So, based on the example given, this couple has a debt-to-income ratio of thirty-five percent and would qualify for the mortgage loan. However, even if your debt-to-income ratio qualifies you for the mortgage loan and the lender says that you can afford the house payment, you do not want to be "mortgage poor"...struggling to pay your mortgage payment. The term "mortgage poor" is discussed further in Chapter Five.

If you decide to add any new debts while your mortgage loan is being processed, the *recalculated* debt-to-income ratio needs to remain less than forty percent in order to qualify for the best rates.

Chapter 3: Documenting Your Income

Being able to verify your income is the next step in the mortgage loan process. **You will need to be able to prove how much income you make on a *regular* and *consistent* basis.** If you are an hourly or salary employee, you will need to have your last two paychecks and the last two years of your W-2 Wage and Tax Statements on hand. If you are an hourly employee and receive any overtime, you will need to be able to prove that the income has been consistent over the last two or more years. Most lenders will not include additional income if it is only seasonal or inconsistent. If you are a salary employee who consistently receives a regular quarterly or yearly bonus, you will need to prove that you receive that extra income on a consistent basis as well. When verifying your income, most lenders or underwriters will look at the year-to-date gross income from your most recent paycheck and then average it with either the last year or two of your W-2 Wage and Tax Statements. **However, it is not a good idea to use any overtime or bonus income to qualify for a loan.** When the overtime is stopped or the bonus income is gone, you might not be able to afford your present debt load or your current standard of living. This could have a damaging effect on your credit rating and your credit score that you worked so hard to build. It is also not a good idea to base your family budget on this extra income.

If you are a "commission only" salesperson, you will need to be able to prove your income in the same manner as the salary employee does. **With commission income, an underwriter is looking for what your *average* income has been over**

the last two or more years, not what your best month or quarter has been. If you have just started a new job and will be paid primarily by commissions or large bonuses, then it would be best to conservatively estimate the income that you will be claiming on the mortgage loan application. If you have just changed professions and started a new job as a commission only employee (i.e., going from a school teacher to a commission real estate agent), then you may have to postpone buying your first house until your income has stabilized and you have been on the job for at least twelve months. In any event, it is always best to apply for a mortgage loan and let the mortgage company review your income situation.

Being self-employed is sometimes a more complicated situation when it comes to verifying your income. One reason is because self-employed people generally fall into two categories based on the way they report their income on their federal tax returns. They can either report the true income (sales) from their business, with the proper deductions and expenses, and pay the proper federal and state income taxes or they can not report the true income, inflate the deductibles and expenses as much as possible, thereby greatly reducing their tax obligations. **As a self-employed borrower, you will qualify for a mortgage loan a lot easier if an underwriter can use your adjusted gross income listed at the bottom of the first page of your 1040 Federal Income Tax Returns.** In some cases, the underwriter will be able to add back to your adjusted gross income any depreciation or interest expense you may have claimed. Depending on the type of business structure you have (Sole Proprietor, Limited Liability Company, or "S" Corporation, to name a few) and if you are attempting to qualify for a conventional mortgage loan, will determine how your federal income tax returns are interpreted. Each lender has an internal analysis on how they review self-employment income and business debt. To reiterate, as a self-employed borrower, you will qualify for the best rates if an underwriter can use the income directly from your federal tax returns with little or no manipulations or adjustments. Therefore, you should have on hand the last two years of your federal tax returns with all schedules along with the last couple of months of business bank statements, in case they are required.

If you "hide" your income in order to avoid paying federal income taxes, then you might have to use an alternative method to prove your income and you might have to search for a non-traditional or unconventional mortgage lender. There are lenders who offer special loan programs that do not require any proof of income, commonly known as "no-doc" loans, or have flexible income requirements. These types of loans come with higher interest rates, generally have higher fees, and will require more for the down payment. Typically, when attempting to qualify for these alternative types of loans, you will need some combination of federal tax returns, bank statements, a financial statement, and a Profit and Loss Statement for you company.

The purpose of the Profit and Loss Statement is to show the mortgage company how your business is performing over the last quarter or last twelve months. To support the gross income, or sales, that you have claimed for the current year on the Profit and Loss Statement, you will need to have your last six to twelve months of business bank statements on hand. The reason the bank statements are important is that they act as your pay stub. Typically, when you receive money from a customer for goods purchased or services rendered, you deposit the money into a particular business checking account similar to a wage earner depositing his regular weekly paycheck. Then the bills are paid from that business checking account. For this reason, it is recommended that you keep separate checking or deposit accounts for your business and your personal use.

An example of a simple Profit and Loss Statement looks like this:

ABC Company
1/1/04 through 8/30/04

Gross Receipts or Sales		$200,000
Cost of Goods Sold (materials)		($85,000)
Gross Profit		$115,000
Expenses		
Wages & Salaries	$40,000	
Automotive Expenses	$15,000	
Other Expenses	$10,000	
Total Expenses		($65,000)
Net Income		$50,000

By law, you do not have to disclose whether you receive any child support or alimony payments unless you need that additional income to qualify for the loan. If you receive child support or alimony from an ex-spouse and you plan on claiming that income in your mortgage application, you will need to be able to prove that you receive the support payments on a *regular* and *consistent* basis. You can make a copy of the last couple of support checks you have received or you can get your last six to twelve months of bank statements together that shows the support income is being consistently received. It is also a good idea to get a copy of the court ordered child support paperwork, or the signed and recorded divorce decree, to add additional support to the income you are claiming. However, you might not be able to use child support income if the dependent will be reaching adult status, typically eighteen years of age, in the near future. Also, alimony income might not be able to be used if the income has certain restrictions such as getting remarried or a termination date that is in the near future.

If you are on a fixed income or you receive a subsidized income (i.e., social security, disability, workman's compensation, or retirement income, to name a few), then you will need to be able to prove how much money you receive on a *monthly* and *consistent* basis and *how long* you will be receiving it. You will need to get your last year's 1099 Federal Wage Form and the most recent award letter or monthly check stub together. If you have direct deposit for this money, then you can use the last two months of your bank statements. Depending on the type of income you receive, you might also have to get a letter from your employer, or from the source of that income, stating how long this income is expected to continue.

By law, you cannot be discriminated against for the type of income you receive. **The key is being able to verify that whatever income you are receiving and using to qualify for the mortgage loan, will be consistently received by you on a** *regular* **and** *ongoing* **basis.** You should never let your income discourage you from applying for a loan. It is always best to apply for the loan, provide proof of your income, and let the mortgage company determine how much income is verifiable and can be used with your loan application.

To summarize documenting your income:
- For an hourly or salary employee, you will need a copy of your last two paychecks and last two years of your W-2 Wage and Tax Statement.
- For a commission sales person, you will need a copy of your last two paychecks and last two years of your W-2 Wage and Tax Statement.
- For a self-employed person qualifying for a conventional mortgage loan, you should have the last two years of your federal tax returns with all schedules along with the last couple months of business bank statements, in case they are required.

- For a self-employed person qualifying for a non-traditional or alternative loan program, you should have the last two years of your federal tax returns with all schedules along with a Profit and Loss Statement, a financial statement, and the last six to twelve months of business bank statements.
- For an individual using child support or alimony income, you will need a copy of the section from the divorce decree which outlines the support payments, a copy of the last two support checks, and the last six months of your bank statements.
- For an individual who receives a fixed or subsidized income, you will need a copy of the most recent award letter, the last year of the 1099 Federal Wage and Tax Form, the last two months of your bank statements, and the last two years of your federal tax returns.

Chapter 4: Applying for the Loan

Now that you have all "your ducks in a row" it is time to find a mortgage lender and prequalify for a mortgage loan. Prequalifying for a mortgage loan is important for a couple of reasons. The first reason is that by prequalifying for the mortgage loan you know you have the ability, income, and credit to buy a house. The second reason is that you will know the price range of houses you will be able to afford. And the third reason is that the real estate agent will be highly motivated in finding you a house knowing that you have been pre-approved for a mortgage loan and that you are serious about buying a home. **It is important that you DO NOT sign a purchase agreement until you know that you have been prequalified for the mortgage loan.**

To find a mortgage company in order to prequalify, I recommend that you contact several mortgage lenders. You will want to compare the mortgage interest rates, prepaid points (commonly known as origination fees) and closing costs (such as processing fee, attorney fee, application fee, document preparation fee, and appraisal fee to name a few). In other words, you need to know how much the loan is going to cost. To find a mortgage lender and company there are a couple sources readily available. You can check the listing of mortgage interest rates in your local newspaper or on the Internet, using "mortgage interest rates" as your key search words. I would also recommend that you contact the local bank where you have your deposit relationship and/or where your checking account is located. If you already know who you will be using as your real estate agent, you can also ask who he or she would recommend as a mortgage loan representative and ask for a rate and fee quote. Choose the lender with whom you are most comfortable and/or gives you the best deal.

Sometimes the lender who offers you the lowest interest rate may not be offering the best overall *value*. A mortgage company may advertise that it offers the lowest interest rate, but then charge more for closing costs and origination fees, thus lessening the appeal as a good value. Some banks will offer you free services such as free checking with direct deposit and/or a free ATM or debit card when you close your mortgage loan with them. This could save you as much as ten to twenty dollars per month in service fees alone. A bank may also be able to offer a discount of their advertised mortgage interest rate by having the new monthly mortgage payment automatically drafted from this new checking account. In addition, you will want to know if your loan will be sold as soon as the mortgage loan is closed. This is important to some people because your mortgage loan could be sold a couple of times within the first two or three years. This may cause you to become confused as to where to mail your mortgage payment. Or the company that the loan is sold to could have a very poor customer service track record.

In order to prequalify for a mortgage loan, you need to complete a mortgage loan application. Completing a loan application is quick and easy if you are prepared to answer the questions. With most companies, you will either complete the loan application in person, over the phone, or even over the Internet. If you complete an application over the phone or the Internet, it is important that the company to which you are applying is a reputable mortgage lender because you are volunteering very valuable information about yourself, such as your social security number and date of birth. If you are applying with a local company over the phone, you can check the local chapter of the Better Business Bureau, ask for references, or check with friends, family, or business associates to make sure that the company is reputable. If you are applying over the Internet, you can check for news articles or investigate the company by searching for their public financial information at any number of financial web sites. If you are not comfortable applying by these methods, then have the company mail you an application.

The mortgage loan application first provides space where you list the last two years worth of your residence information and for whom you have worked. When giving the dates of residency or employment, you do not need to know the exact day, but only the month and year. For your housing information, you will need to provide the street address(es) where you have lived over the last two years. If you rented, you will need to provide the landlord's name and how the mortgage company can contact that person in case they need to verify your rental payments. For your work information, you will need to provide information for whom you have worked over the last two years. You will need to list the phone number or mailing address to the place of business in case the work information needs to be verified. The application has space to show details about your income (you gathered this information in Chapter Three). You will then need to provide a list of all your assets: (1) How much money is in your checking and/or savings account, (2) how much money you have in any retirement or investment accounts, (3) how many and what type of automobile(s) you own, and their approximate values, and (4) any other miscellaneous property or asset you may own with its approximate value will need to be listed. The application has space for you to provide details about what debts you owe and how much you pay each month for those debts. If you are well prepared, then filling out the mortgage application will only take about ten to fifteen minutes and the loan officer will be able to get started immediately in prequalifying you for a mortgage loan. Not being able to completely answer all questions will cause an unnecessary delay in the mortgage loan process.

With each application you complete to prequalify for a mortgage loan, each lender is required to give you, within three business days, an early disclosure package of information if they have not declined your application. This early disclosure package will have a lot of information in it. You need to read through the material carefully and ask questions about anything you do not understand. **The two most important early disclosure forms are the Good Faith Estimate and the Preliminary Truth in Lending Disclosure.** The Good Faith Estimate will disclose and list what the estimated closing costs will be. The Preliminary Truth in Lending will list the estimated mortgage payment and interest rate. These are the two forms you can use to compare the different mortgage loan proposals you will be receiving. Shopping around and filling out two or three mortgage loan applications could potentially cause a slight drop in your credit score, if these different lenders each pull your credit report. However, the point drop caused by having a couple of inquiries within a day or two will be very minimal, if any at all.

Points for you to review in the pre-disclosure packages are:

- What is the interest rate?
- What is the principle and interest mortgage payment?

- What is the loan origination fee?
- What are the total closing costs?
- What is the total cost of the loan (including principle loan amount, finance charge, and closing costs)?
- Is there a prepayment penalty?
- Is this a 30 year fixed rate loan or some other type?

Write the answers down on paper and compare them closely. This will help you to choose the mortgage loan officer and the company with whom you will do your mortgage loan. After you have chosen the mortgage lender and loan officer, it is important that you contact any other lenders you may have applied with and withdraw your loan application from consideration. **You can only have one mortgage application pending at one time.**

Once you have decided on a mortgage company and lender, you will be required to sign and return the early disclosure package you initially received along with the required documents as requested by the lender. Some of the required documents may include: Proof of income, verification of rent, proof of your down payment, and a credit explanation letter for any slow pay history or bankruptcy discharge papers, if applicable. Remember to keep a copy of the pre-disclosure package for yourself so you can refer to it later.

Summary of documents required by lender:
- Signed and returned mortgage application
- Signed and returned early disclosure package
- Proof of income
- Verification of rent
- Proof of down payment

- A credit explanation letter for any late payments or credit blemishes and bankruptcy discharge papers, if applicable.

Remember, if thirty days passes from the time the lender initially pulled your credit report for prequalification until you actually close your loan, the lender might request another credit report prior to closing. At this stage, the loan could still be denied if anything has changed. So, it is important that you do not inquire anywhere for credit until *after* you sign the new loan note.

Chapter 5: The Thirty-Year Mortgage Loan

For typical first time home buyers, the general recommendation is to keep the loan terms simple and get a thirty-year fixed rate mortgage loan. With this type of mortgage loan, the interest rate and monthly payments remain the same for the entire loan. The reasons why this type of mortgage loan is most recommended are that it is the easiest loan to understand and the most popular loan product. However, if your income can support a higher mortgage payment, then you could opt for a shorter-term fixed rate mortgage loan such as a fifteen or twenty-year loan. The reason is that a shorter term mortgage loan will save you a lot of money over the life of the loan in total finance charges (interest) when compared to the thirty-year fixed rate mortgage loan.

There are other types of mortgage loan products available if you know you are only going to be in your house for a short period of time. Other types of mortgage loans are: An A.R.M. (Adjustable Rate Mortgage) Loan, a Balloon Loan, or a Negative Amortization Loan. (These different types of mortgage loans are explained in more detail in Section Two, Chapter Four.) The A.R.M. Loan is a combination of the

Fixed Rate Mortgage Loan and a variable interest rate loan. The key difference is that after the fixed rate period expires, the loan becomes a variable interest rate loan and the monthly payment could increase dramatically over time as determined by your agreement with the lender. The Balloon Loan is similar to an A.R.M. Loan except that after the fixed rate period expires, the remaining principle loan balance is due and must be paid. A Negative Amortization Loan is an alternative loan that is only good in an area where property values are increasing at a very high rate. You can also discuss these other loan products with the mortgage loan officer whom you have chosen.

When selecting the thirty-year mortgage loan, because of the low fixed monthly payment it offers, there is still a way to save money without being locked into a higher monthly payment as with a shorter-term mortgage loan. A great way to save lots of money is to always pay an extra principle amount with each monthly payment. The resulting savings over the life of the loan by doing this can be very substantial. Consider this, for a thirty-year $150,000 mortgage loan, paying extra principle could reduce the length of the loan by five or more years and would save you well over $50,000 in finance charges!

There are several ways to pay extra principle. The first way is to pay an extra amount, whether its ten dollars or two hundred dollars, with each mortgage payment…whatever you can afford based on your monthly family budget. A second way is to pay a thirteenth payment at the end of each calendar year. A third way to save money in total finance charges is to pay half of your mortgage payment every two weeks, which will also equal thirteen annualized payments.
If you choose the second or third way to save money, then you need to verify the repayment plan with the mortgage company to make sure that the extra payment is allowed. **The key to saving money by paying extra principle is that you must be**

consistent and *always* note on the monthly statement or payment coupon that the extra amount is to be applied to the *principle* balance. If you don't tell the mortgage company that the extra money is to pay down the principle, then it will probably be placed in your escrow account. The best part about using one of the three methods listed is that you will not be *contractually obligated* to pay extra every month. And unlike a shorter mortgage term, you will not be locked into a higher monthly mortgage payment. **Any time you can send extra money to reduce the principle balance, the greater your savings will be over the life of the loan.**

The Escrow Account

Along with the thirty-year mortgage loan, it is recommended that the monthly mortgage payment include an escrow payment for the yearly real estate taxes and the annual homeowner's insurance premium. The escrow account is as if the mortgage company is keeping a savings account for you in order to collect money to pay these bills. You deposit money into the escrow account each month from part of the monthly mortgage payment. When these bills come due, the mortgage company pays the bill from this savings, or escrow, account. There are two main reasons why an escrow account is popular. The first reason is that most people are not disciplined enough to put money into a regular savings account on a consistent and monthly basis. The second reason is that other people will chose to escrow for these bills for the convenience, such as myself. Most all mortgage companies do not charge a fee for this service, so to escrow money does not cost you anything.

The first bill that the escrow account pays is the real estate taxes owed on the property. The real estate taxes you pay on your house are collected by and paid to the city, town, or county where your house is located to help fund the local government. These taxes must be paid in a timely manner or a lien can be placed against your home. If a lien is placed on your home due to non-payment, then the local government has a right to foreclose on your house in order to satisfy these delinquent property taxes. Also, if the mortgage company fails to pay your real estate taxes, then you are still liable for payment. This is why you want to choose a reputable mortgage company with a good customer service track record.

The second bill is for the annual homeowner's insurance premium. Homeowner's insurance is a requirement of the mortgage loan by the mortgage company. It protects your most expensive asset, your home, in case it is destroyed or damaged. If something happens to your house, then the homeowner's insurance policy will pay to repair the damage or cost to fix your home so that it is as good as new. If you did not have any homeowner's insurance and your house was destroyed, you would still be responsible for repaying the debt to the mortgage company. The whole loan balance would be owed and would have to be repaid to the mortgage company at the time the collateral was destroyed. If the mortgage lender does not pay your insurance premium in a timely manner, then you will be responsible for paying the insurance premium out of pocket.

A third possible cost that could be added to the monthly escrow payment is mortgage insurance, also known as private mortgage insurance or PMI. If you are financing more than eighty percent of the purchase price or value of the home and you are getting a conventional mortgage loan, then this will be a required insurance. The mortgage insurance protects the mortgage company from any loss they might incur (should you default on your mortgage loan) because it agreed to lend you more than the eighty-percent loan-to-value benchmark. "Loan-to-value" is simply the mortgage loan amount you are borrowing divided by the value of the property. Because of this insurance, mortgage companies can afford to lend first time home buyers close to one hundred percent of the sales price of the home. This makes home ownership available to almost everybody.

If you want to avoid paying the mortgage insurance premium, you can opt for a first mortgage/second mortgage combination loan (also known as an "80/10/10", "80/15/5", or "80/20" loan) which is discussed in more detail in Section Three, Chapter One. The combination loan means that the first mortgage loan would be for the loan amount equal to eighty percent ("80") of the purchase price of the home. The second number represents what the second mortgage loan balance would be as a percentage of the purchase price of the home, either ten percent ("10"), fifteen percent ("15"), or twenty percent ("20"). The third number represents the amount of cash, as a percentage of the purchase price, that you would be putting down as the down payment on the house you are buying, either ten percent ("10"), five percent ("5"), or zero percent. The two reasons people choose to avoid this insurance product are because the money paid towards this monthly insurance premium is not tax deductible and the insurance doesn't pay a benefit directly to the homeowner. Remember to check with your lender to see if they have any restrictions on getting a second mortgage loan. Also, the combined monthly payment could be a little higher than the one mortgage payment, so make sure the two payments fit in your family budget.

Mortgage Poor

The last step with the thirty-year mortgage loan is to make sure that you can afford the mortgage payment. You do not want to buy your first house and be "mortgage poor". Being "mortgage poor" means that you have a house payment that you can barely afford after all the monthly loan payments, utility bills, and grocery bills have been paid, to truly *enjoy* your house. The mortgage loan officer will tell you, after applying for a loan, that you have been pre-approved to borrow up to "X" amount. You need to ask the mortgage loan officer to calculate a range of possible mortgage payments based on the pre-approved loan amount. **You want to make sure that you can afford the mortgage payment based on *your* family budget and not *their* assessment of your ability to pay.**

As an example, let's say that you were pre-approved to borrow up to $200,000 at 7.5% for 30 years. That is the maximum amount the mortgage company will approve for you based on your debt-to-income ratio. The principle and interest payment associated with that loan amount would be $1,400 per month. You would then ask the loan officer what the monthly principle and interest payment would be for homes costing $160,000, $170,000, $180,000, and $190,000. **This would give you a range of payments in order for you to determine what monthly payment would work best with *your* family budget.** As a reminder, when you figure your family budget you need to make sure that the proposed mortgage payment includes the escrow payment amount because the escrow portion could add a couple of hundred dollars to the proposed monthly payment. The $1,400 principle and interest payment could potentially become a $1,700 or $1,800 monthly mortgage payment after the escrow payment is added.

The estimated escrow payment should be disclosed, along with the principle and interest payment, in the Early Truth In Lending Disclosure provided by the lender. If not, calculating how much your escrow account will add to your monthly mortgage payment is an easy process. For this example, the house you want costs $150,000 and you will be borrowing $135,000 at 8%. Therefore, the loan-to-value ratio is 90%.

$135,000 Loan Balance
÷150,000 Purchase Price
   90%   Loan-to-value Ratio

The real estate taxes for this example are $1.50 per each $100 of assessed property value. To find this information, you would contact the local city or county tax assessor's office for the area where you are looking to live. Therefore, in this example the real estate taxes will add an additional $187.50 per month to the mortgage payment! That is a significant amount of money.

$150,000 Purchase Price $1,500.00
÷100.00 Of Value   x $1.50 Tax Assessed Value
$1,500.00   ÷ 12 Months
                            $187.50 Per Month added to Escrow

The homeowner's insurance annual premium will cost you approximately $500.00 per year for this example. You can obtain an insurance quote or estimate by contacting the same insurance agent with whom you have your auto or renter's insurance, by using your parent's insurance agent, or by looking for agents in the phone book or on the internet. Getting back to our example, the homeowner's insurance premium will add $41.67 per month to the mortgage payment.

$500.00 Annual Premium
÷ 12 Months
$41.67 Per Month added to Escrow

Because you are financing more than eighty percent of the value of the home, the mortgage insurance premium will cost you $.65 per $1,000 of the property value. You will have to get this insurance premium quote from your mortgage loan officer because the monthly premium varies for several reasons: by the company, your credit score, and actual loan-to-value. So, in this example, the mortgage insurance premium (or PMI) will add $87.75 per month to the mortgage payment.

$135,000 Loan Balance	$135.00
÷1,000.00 Of Value	x $.65 PMI Value
$135.00	$87.75 Per Month added to Escrow

Your principle and interest mortgage payment for this example is $991. After you add in the escrow payment of $316.92, the actual monthly mortgage payment increases to $1,307.92. Wow!

    $991.00 Principle & Interest Payment
 + $187.50 Real Estate Taxes
 + $41.67 Homeowner's Insurance
 + $87.75 Mortgage Insurance
  $1,307.92 Total Monthly Mortgage Pmt

You need to make sure that *this* payment (that includes the extras) is the payment that fits into your family budget. If this payment is too much, you need to either put more money down or buy a lower priced house. Remember, you want to be able to enjoy your first house.

Chapter 6: House Hunting

To find a good real estate agent, I would start by getting advice from friends, relatives, and coworkers who live in the same geographical area in which you are interested. It is important to find a real estate agent who is familiar with the area because a local agent will be better able to inform you more about the neighborhoods and/or subdivisions, about the school systems, about the demographics, etc. Before you choose a real estate agent, I suggest that you interview the agent to try and determine how professional he or she is. This can be done over the phone or in person at their office. A couple of questions to ask the agent:

- How long have you been a *licensed* real estate agent?
- Do you do this full-time or part-time?
- What is your educational background?
- Do you live in the area?
- Why do you enjoy being a real estate agent?
- Do you have any references?

After you have interviewed the agent, the next step is to have the agent take you on a short trip around the area so you can determine how well the real estate agent really knows the location. By doing this, you can see if communication between you and the agent is good. You need to be able to *trust* the agent and get your questions *answered* honestly.

In any case, the real estate agent you choose will be impressed with your preparation because you read this book, have answers to probable questions, have your relevant financial documents handy, and have already been pre-approved for a mortgage loan. The agent will be very motivated to find you a house because he or she knows that you are serious about buying a home. When discussing homes with the agent during the interview process, it is best to let the person know what price range you are comfortable with. **If the mortgage lender approved you for up to a $200,000 loan but you feel that your family budget works best in the $170,000 to $180,000 range, then you should be looking at houses priced in that range only.** If the agent seems to be showing you houses priced above your comfortable requested range, then it is best that you interview another real estate agent.

In order for the business relationship to be successful, there needs to be good, open communication between you and the agent. The real estate agent needs to know and understand what type of property you are looking for and where this property should be located. **The first key bit of information that the real estate agent needs to**

understand is what type of house you are looking for. You need to be able to briefly describe the key characteristics and features of the house and property such as the questions listed below that my wife and I discussed as being important to us.

- Do you want a large yard or a small yard?
- Does the yard need to be fenced?
- Do you have any pets or small children?
- How many bedrooms and bathrooms do you prefer?
- Do you prefer a one-story or a two-story house?
- Do you want a newer home or an older, established house?
- Do you want city water and sewer or is well and septic all right?

You should make a list of your own questions and answers for what key characteristics and features are most important to you. These questions will help you to describe the house to the real estate agent.

The second key bit of information is to know the area or location where you want to live. The questions below are some of the ones my wife and I discussed prior to meeting with our real estate agent.

- Do you want to live in a planned community or subdivision?
- Live in the city limits, or live in the country?
- Do you want to be near schools or shopping centers?
- Do you want to live near where you work, near a highway, or public transportation?

You should make a list of your own questions and answers for the area and location where you want to live that are most important to you. These questions will help you describe the area and location of the house to the real estate agent.

After you find a compatible agent, you may be encouraged to sign a Buyer's Agreement. A Buyer's Agreement simply states that you choose this real estate agent to *exclusively* represent you for a period of time while you are house hunting.

However, in some states you are not required to sign this agreement. If your state requires you to sign this agreement, or you are more comfortable doing so, then you would only want to commit exclusively to this agent for a short period of time, usually no more than thirty to sixty days. This will benefit you in three ways. The first way is that the agent should be more motivated to find you a house that meets your needs knowing that the exclusive arrangement is not long term. Secondly, if you get a real estate agent who is just not working well with you, then you are not exclusively bound to the agent for an extended period of time. And lastly, as your buyer's agent, the realtor is obligated to answer more detailed questions about the property.

Most real estate purchase transactions will cost the seller between five-percent and six-percent of the purchase price as the realtor's commission fee if the seller decides to use a realtor. This fee is evenly divided between the seller's real estate agency and the buyer's real estate agency, if there are two agents involved. Sometimes, you can negotiate a deal for less if you agree to purchase a house where the real estate agent is also the listing agent, which means he or she is also the agent who is also selling the house. And sometimes you can save commission fees if you buy a house directly from a builder or an individual selling the house as "for sale by owner" (F.S.B.O.). If you do decide to buy a house directly from a builder, then it would be a good idea to check the builder's references to verify that you are getting a house that is well built and properly priced.

Chapter 7: Understanding the Loan Approval Process

You have now been preapproved for a mortgage loan and have found a house. Great job! You are almost there. The hard parts have already been completed. It is now time to get final approval for your mortgage loan. While you were house hunting, the mortgage company or bank was busy verifying your job(s), your deposit accounts, your rent payments, and your credit references. The mortgage underwriter might choose to request another credit report prior to final approval, so remember it is important that you do not apply for credit anywhere until after you close your mortgage loan. **Also, remember not to spend a significant amount of your remaining cash because there might be an unexpected bill or two.** An unexpected bill or additional cost could be caused by a slight increase in closing costs, unforeseen moving expenses, minor repairs or cosmetic improvements to the house that you are buying, or repairs to the house or apartment that you are moving from.

After you have negotiated the sale price, possibly with the help of a realtor, and signed a sales contract, the eight tasks listed below will need to be completed before you can actually close on the mortgage loan. This process should take less than thirty days. Be patient, you are almost in your home! Your mortgage loan officer and real estate agent will take care of most of these tasks and can also explain in more detail, if needed, what each item represents. **The cost for these services has already been included in and disclosed to you by the Good Faith Estimate,** which is a part of the pre-disclosure package the mortgage lender was required to give to you at the time you completed the mortgage loan application. You have the option of choosing whomever you want for these services, but usually the realtor or mortgage loan officer has companies or individuals lined up that you can choose from to perform these assigned tasks. These companies are more inclined to give preferential treatment and speedy service to your realtor or mortgage loan officer because they get repeat business from them.

The Eight Elements of Loan Closing

The first is an appraisal which will need to be performed on the property that you are interested in buying. This will determine what the true market value of the home is as compared to the listing price. The appraisal will compare the home to similar homes in the neighborhood or the surrounding geographical area. The goal for the appraiser is to match the home that you are interested in with recent sales of similar homes and compare these prices. The appraiser tries to find at least three comparable homes and then analyzes the similarities and differences and equates a dollar figure for each adjustment. The appraiser will come up with a dollar figure for what the current market conditions indicate that the house is worth. Make sure the appraiser is licensed to do business in your state and that you get a copy of the appraisal report with your loan-closing package.

Second, a survey will need to be performed of the land on which the house sits. This is not a service that should be taken lightly or not performed because it is important that you know your boundary lines and how much land is rightfully yours. The surveyor will draw your property lines and any easements or "right-of-ways" that might be associated with your property. An easement, or right-of-way, is the legal permission for a company or person to use that part of your land. Utility companies will have easements typically in the front or back of your yard in order to run any number of utility lines such as water and sewer, electric, cable, or phone service. A right-of-way could also be for a neighbor to use part of your land to gain access to his land that is along side or behind your land. A right-of-way could be for the county or town to widen the road that borders your property. The surveyor will mark your land with little temporary flags so that when you first move into your home you will be able to tell exactly where your property lines are. If permanent metal rods are not buried in the ground where these little temporary flags are, I would recommend that you have the surveyor put those permanent markers in place at the property line points. You will want to make sure that a licensed and professional surveyor performs this service and that you get a copy of the survey report with your loan-closing package.

The third thing that needs to be done to the house you are buying is a termite inspection. The termite inspection needs to be performed unless you are buying a newly constructed, just completed house. **The termite inspection is very important because you need to make sure that the house you are buying is not infested with any type of wood eating insects; such as termites or carpenter ants.** Therefore, only a state licensed exterminator should perform the inspection. You will want to retain a copy of the termite inspection report after it is completed and prior to closing your loan. If there are any detected wood destroying insects or there is damaged wood found, then the seller of the house must pay to have the bugs eliminated and the wood repaired or replaced.

Fourth, I recommend that you have a home inspection performed on the house you are buying. Even if you are buying a house in "as-is" condition, it is still a good idea to have a home inspection performed. The report would give you an independent opinion as to the structural condition of the house and what repairs to the house would be deemed most important and should be tackled first. The home inspector's main purpose is to detect any visual defects of the house. You will want to be present when the home inspection is being performed. The home inspector will check all the utilities to make sure they are in working order, look underneath the house and in the attic for any defects or watermarks. A good home inspector will also give you advice on how to properly maintain the home. For these reasons, I recommend that you walk around the house with the inspector. You will want to make sure that the inspector is well qualified to do the inspection. Some states require that the inspector be licensed as well. You should get a copy of the home inspection report prior to closing your loan. If the report indicates that the home has defects or recommended repairs, you will need to negotiate with the seller on what repairs need to be done and who will pay for them, unless you are buying the property in "as-is" condition. Some of the repairs or cosmetic improvements recommended by the home inspector will be minor. These will be your responsibility to pay for. You'll have to determine if the house is worth it.

The fifth thing is for the mortgage company to have a flood search performed on the actual physical location of your house. Flood searches are a federal requirement on all mortgage loan transactions where a structure is involved. The purpose of the report is to check to see if the house you are buying is located in a flood zone. If the home is in a designated flood plain, you will have to buy flood insurance. The flood insurance premium can be very expensive. It is necessary to have flood insurance because the standard homeowner's insurance policy will not insure your house against any damages caused by a flood.

The sixth thing that will be done by either a title search company or the attorney, who will be doing the loan closing, is to perform a title search on the property at the local courthouse where the property is located. The purpose of the title search is to check and make sure that you are buying the house from the legal owners. The search will also verify that there are no other liens, judgments or encumbrances that might jeopardize the marketability of the house. **It is important that you get title insurance with the search of the property.** Title insurance will guarantee your ownership rights and protect you in case any errors or omissions are later found.

This will protect you from any old liens, judgments, or encumbrances that might show up on any future title searches against the previous owners. This is especially important when you try to later sell the house. Therefore, make sure that you get a copy of the insurance binder at the loan closing, or shortly thereafter, from the closing attorney once the policy binder has been completed. **The insurance binder will be your written proof of ownership (along with the Deed of Trust) and clear title to the property purchased.**

The seventh thing required is that you have homeowner's insurance in place before you close on your mortgage loan. It is best that you start interviewing insurance agents as you start your house hunting. I recommend that you shop around and get at least three insurance rate quotes. The first place to check is your auto insurance company because most will give you a discount for having both your auto and homeowner's insurance with them. Another good source is to contact the insurance agent that your parents, siblings, or close friends use. You will want to make sure that the company you select has a good reputation, pays its claims in a timely manner and is financially sound. Also make sure the homeowner's insurance policy you select has full coverage and comes with "replacement cost". Replacement cost means that if your house is damaged or destroyed, that it will be repaired using *today's* cost, (i.e., what it would take to rebuild the house in today's market) not what it cost to originally build.

The eighth and final thing (depending on where you are buying your house) is that you may want to check with the local government's zoning board or planning board to see what **the long range growth plans are for the geographical area where the house is located.** You can find out where to get this information at the town hall. You will want to check the future growth maps to see how road improvements or future planned developments might affect the house and property value. The state's ten or twenty year growth plan might include building a large bypass highway around the city, which could come within one hundred yards of the home's property line. Another potential problem is vacant land that is zoned for commercial use. A manufacturing plant could potentially be built near the home which would add a lot of traffic and increased truck use on the roads in your neighborhood. You would not know about these future potential land uses unless you checked the public records. Your neighborhood could get very noisy and congested causing your property value to decrease. The quality of life that you were seeking when you bought your house could be greatly diminished if the records contain future plans that are undesirable to you. You will also want to find out if there are any impending (tax) assessments for public works projects, such as adding sidewalks or connecting your house to the town water and sewage lines that you would be responsible for.

Chapter 8: Ready to Close the Deal

The loan is ready to be closed when the information from your loan application has been verified and all necessary reports have been completed. **You should go over the final figures with your mortgage loan officer a day or two prior to going to the closing table.** This review prevents any surprises or last minute changes. If there are any changes, then you will want to take care of them before you get to the closing table. **If there are any surprises, or if you uncover anything that you do not agree with, DO NOT SIGN the paperwork.** The loan papers constitute a legal money transaction and, once signed, there is no rescission or cancellation period. You have two choices if you uncover any discrepancies or surprises. You can either (1) negotiate and settle the problem or (2) void the sales contact. If you void the sale contract and decide to walk away from the table, then you will most likely forfeit your deposit that you put down (as a sign of good faith) when you agreed to the sales contract. But this is a small price to pay for the much larger mortgage loan contract that you would have been stuck with.

When reviewing the paperwork, pay close attention to the final Settlement Statement. **Make sure all charges and fees listed are very close to what you initially agreed to when you applied for the loan.** You can do this by comparing the charges listed on the final Settlement Statement with the estimated closing cost listed in the Good Faith Estimate that you received when you applied for the loan. It is also important to review the Final Truth in Lending (the promissory note) Statement. You should check this form to make sure the total monthly payment, which should include the monthly escrow charges, is what you were expecting. This form should also indicate when the first payment is due. Lastly, check the Deed of Trust to make sure that your name is properly spelled and that the property has been correctly identified.

CONGRATULATIONS!!

Section II
Refinancing Your Mortgage Loan

Introduction

Section Two is specifically written for the homeowner who is considering refinancing his or her current first mortgage. This section will help you in four major ways. First it will help you determine if you should refinance. Second, it will educate you on how to qualify for the mortgage loan. Third, it will let you know what types of mortgage loans are available. Fourth, it will serve as a guide through the mortgage refinance process. This section also offers tips and pointers to help you become a more educated and savvy borrower.

Chapter 1: To Refinance or Not To Refinance

There are a variety of reasons why people choose to refinance their first mortgage loan. The two most popular reasons to refinance are: (1) To lower their current interest rate and (2) to save money. But there are also certain times when it does not make good financial sense to refinance. To refinance or not to refinance is the big question. This chapter will discuss when it makes good financial sense to refinance based on the two most popular reasons stated above.

Refinance and Lower the Interest Rate

One reason people choose to refinance their first mortgage loan is to *lower* their interest rate. The interest rate on a mortgage loan gotten a couple of years ago could be higher or lower than what is being offered today. That is because interest rates are always fluctuating and changing along with changes in the economy. In any event, you now have the opportunity to lower your interest rate.

Now might also be a good time to refinance if you had to accept an undesirable interest rate at the time of your original mortgage loan due to bad credit or a low credit score. However, after you read Section Five of this book, you will be able to improve your credit score to where you will be able to qualify for the preferred mortgage interest rate!

A popular belief is that if you can get a mortgage interest rate that is at least one percentage point less than the interest rate you currently have on your mortgage loan, then you should automatically refinance. This is *sometimes* a true statement that requires investigation and analysis. You will need to access an amortization table for the examples listed. You can find an amortization table at a number of financial websites or go to our website **www.theborrowingmoneyguide.com** for links to one.

As an example, let's follow along with Troy and Shannon Walker as they discuss refinancing their mortgage loan. The Walkers are a young couple who just purchased their first house eighteen months ago. They originally took out a $150,000 mortgage loan at 9% for 30 years as first time home buyers. They have talked it over and agree that they plan on remaining in the house for at least the next seven or eight years, until they have started a family. Looking at their original loan paperwork, Shannon finds that the total finance charge (interest) for their current thirty-year mortgage loan at 9% is $284,500. Now, a year and a half later, mortgage rates have dropped to 8%. Shannon figures that now is a good time to refinance. Having been in the house for only a short period of time, Shannon assumes that their mortgage balance has not gone down much. So she goes to an amortization table and finds that a new thirty-year mortgage loan at 8% for $150,000 will cost only $246,200 over thirty years. Shannon is very excited to tell Troy that they can save a total of $38,300 in finance charges over the life of the loan! She wants to refinance. On the surface, this appears to be a good decision.

$284,500 Total Finance Charge, 9% for 30 years
-246,200 Total Finance Charge, 8% for 30 years
$38,300 Total Savings over *30 years*

But Troy decides to look a little closer. Troy calls the mortgage company and finds out that their actual principle mortgage loan balance is now down to $148,400. Looking at the amortization table, Troy sees that over the last eighteen months they have paid a total of $20,100 in finance charges (or interest). Troy does a little bit of calculating and determines that the *remaining cost* (finance charge) of their original mortgage loan at 9% is actually only $264,400.

$284,500 Finance Charge at 9% for 30 year Loan
-20,100 Interest Paid to Date on Loan
$264,400 Remaining Finance Charge at 9%

Shannon then goes back to the amortization table and finds that refinancing their current principle balance amount of $148,400 at 8% for 30 years will actually cost a total of $243,600 in finance charges (interest). Next, Shannon calls around to a couple of mortgage lenders and determines that refinancing their mortgage loan would cost them approximately $2,350.00. The closing cost includes a one percent origination fee, an appraisal fee, title search fee, attorney fee, and recording fee to record the deed of trust. Adding in the closing cost, Troy calculates that the total cost of a new mortgage loan would be approximately $245,950.

> $243,600 Total Finance Charge, 8% for 30 years
> +2,350 Estimated Closing Cost to Refinance
> $245,950 Total Cost of New Loan,8% for 30 years

Shannon recalculates the actual cost savings with refinancing their mortgage loan for **another thirty years** and finds that the actual savings is $18,450.

> $264,400 Remaining Finance Charge at 9%
> -245,950 Total Cost of New Loan, 8% for 30 years
> $18,450 *Actual* Total Savings over *30 years*

So, Shannon informs Troy that the $38,300 in savings that she thought they had is actually only $18,450...but still well worth refinancing. In this example it would be a good decision for the Walkers to refinance, provided they are going to remain in their house for at least the next seven years (this will be discussed further in the next few pages).

Now, let's look at another example using the same scenario. If you remember, Troy and Shannon Walker had originally taken out a $150,000 mortgage loan at 9%. The total finance charges for this loan cost them approximately $284,500 over thirty years. Suppose that the Walkers, for whatever reason, chose not to refinance back when they had the opportunity to do so and have now lived in their house for *nine* years. They still have *twenty-one* years left to pay on the original thirty-year mortgage loan. They now have two children, ages five and three. The Walkers like the neighborhood and the school system and have decided to remain in their house for another seven or eight years. They are now ready to refinance and the mortgage rates are back down to 8%. Troy calls the mortgage company and finds out that their principle mortgage balance is now down to $136,500. Troy utilizes the website of this book (**www.theborrowingmoneyguide.com**) to find a link to an amortization table. Looking at the amortization table for the $150,000 loan at 9%, and scrolling down to 108 months (9 years x 12 months), the table shows that the Walkers have paid approximately $116,800 in interest to date. Troy then calculates that the remaining cost of their original 9% mortgage loan is $167,700.

> $284,500 Total Finance Charge, 9% for 30 years
> -116,800 Interest Paid to Date on Loan
> $167,700 *Remaining* Finance Charge at *9%*

Troy then looks up their current principle balance of $136,500 at 8% and determines from the amortization table that it would cost a total of $224,000 in interest (finance charges) to refinance for *another thirty years*. Shannon calls around to a couple of lenders and finds that the closing cost to refinance is a little bit less than before. The total closing costs are approximately $2,150.00, which includes a one percent origination fee, an appraisal fee, title search fee, attorney fee, and recording fee to record the deed of trust. So, Shannon is able to calculate that the total cost of a new thirty-year mortgage loan would be $226,150.

> $224,000 Total Finance Charge, 8% for 30 years
> +2,150 Estimated Closing Cost to Refinance
> $226,150 Total Cost of New Mortgage, *8%* for 30 years

Shannon tells Troy that, surprisingly, even though interest rates have dropped by one full percentage point, **refinancing the mortgage loan back to *thirty years* will actually *cost* $58,450 in finance charges.**

> $226,150 Total Cost of New Mortgage, 8% for 30 years
> -167,700 Remaining Finance Charge at 9%
> $58,450 *Additional* Cost if Refinanced for *30 years*

This example shows that the old adage of "if you can reduce your interest rate by one percent then you should automatically refinance" does not hold true... and can actually end up costing you more money in the long run!

Shannon thinks there has to be a way to save money since interest rates have fallen by one percentage point. Shannon then remembers (from reading Section One of this book) when they first bought their house, that Chapter Four discussed **saving money by getting a** *shorter-term* **mortgage term.** In example one, the Walkers had over *twenty-eight* years remaining to pay on their mortgage loan. In example two, the Walkers had only *twenty-one* years remaining to pay. **The two keys to determining if you should refinance your mortgage loan: (1) Know how much time you have left to pay on your current mortgage loan and (2) how much interest (finance charge) is left to be paid.** You need to be able to determine how much interest (finance charge) is remaining on the original mortgage loan in order to determine if refinancing will actually save you money. This is especially important if you have lived in your house for more than seven years. **A lot of people make the mistake of automatically assuming that they have to get another** *thirty-year* **mortgage loan.**

Shannon and Troy continue to discuss their dilemma. And in this third example, Shannon comes up with the idea that they should look *at refinancing for the approximate time remaining* on their mortgage loan. Shannon says to Troy, "We know that we have paid on our mortgage loan for 9 years, so there are twenty-one years left to pay. What do you think might happen if we try to refinance our mortgage loan for only twenty years?" Troy goes to the amortization table and sees that $136,500 at 8% would only cost $137,500 in finance charges over 20 years. The closing cost would again cost approximately $2,150.00. So the total cost of a new twenty-year mortgage loan would be only $139,650.

$137,500 Total Finance Charge, 8% for 20 years
+2,150 Estimated Closing Cost to Refinance
$139,650 Total Cost of New Mortgage, 8% for 20 years

Remembering back from the previous example that the remaining finance charge on the original mortgage loan at 9% was $167,700, Shannon excitedly tells Troy, "So by **refinancing our mortgage loan for only the approximate *remaining* term** of twenty years, the new mortgage loan saves us $28,050 in finance charges. Let's refinance!"

$167,700 Remaining Finance Charge, 9%
-139,650 Total Cost of New Mortgage, 8% for 20 years
$28,050 *Total Savings* if Refinanced for *20 years*

So, in this example the old adage holds true that "you should refinance if interest rates drop by one percent" as long as you **refinance for no more than the remaining term of your original mortgage loan** and you plan on remaining in your house for more than seven years. To save even more money, some borrowers will refinance for only a fifteen-year term. This will increase your total savings even more, but remember it will also increase your monthly principle and interest payment.

The Break Even Point

What if you wanted to refinance your mortgage loan because it passed the test in the first set of examples, but you knew you would not be in your house for more than seven years? Should you still refinance? Again, some people will say that if you can lower your interest rate by one full percentage point that you should automatically refinance. But that is not always the correct answer. The correct answer is contingent upon: (1) How you answer two important questions below and

(2) calculating where the break-even point is in terms of actually saving money.
The break even point is the point at which the monthly savings between the old and new monthly mortgage payment *equals* **the closing cost of the new mortgage loan.** It is the point at which you actually start to save money.

These are the two important questions to answer: (1) How long will I be living in my house and (2) how much money will it cost me to refinance? You need to be honest with yourself and figure out how long you plan to be in your current home. Some other questions are important to consider as well.

* Is there a good chance you might get relocated with your work?
* Are you planning to start a family and will need a bigger house in the very near future?
* Will you be getting a raise or a promotion that makes you able to afford a larger house as a reward?
* Will you be retiring in the next couple of years and downsizing to a smaller house?

To find the break even point of where you actually start to save money by refinancing depends on how much the closing cost will be to refinance compared to exactly how much money you will be saving each month with your new *principle and interest* mortgage payment. Let's suppose that your present mortgage balance is again $150,000. The current interest on your mortgage loan is now 8%. In the first example, the current mortgage interest rate has dropped a half of a percentage point to 7.5%. In the second example, the current mortgage interest rate has dropped a full percentage point to 7%. You have inquired with your local bank and a couple of local mortgage lenders and the consensus is that it will cost you approximately $2,350.00 in closing costs to refinance your mortgage loan. Looking at an amortization table, your principle and interest mortgage payment at 8% is $1,100.00.

The principle and interest mortgage payment at 7.5% equals $1,049.00 (an apparent savings of $51.00 per month) and at 7% the principle and interest mortgage payment is only $998.00 (an apparent savings of $102.00 per month). Before making a decision to refinance solely based on these figures, calculate the break-even point. In the two examples listed below, we will look at calculating the break-even point using monthly payments.

Example 1: Mortgage rates have fallen by a *half of a percentage point.*

$1,100.00 Mortgage Pmt, 8% $2,350.00 Closing Cost, New Mortgage
-1,049.00 Mortgage Pmt, 7.5%   ÷ 51.00 Monthly Savings
   $51.00 Monthly Savings   46 Months Break Even Point

Month	8% PMT	7.5% PMT	Monthly Savings	Closing Cost	Monthly Savings	Break Even Point
1	$1,100	$1,049	$51	$2,350	$51	$2,299
2	$1,100	$1,049	$51	$2,299	$51	$2,248
3	$1,100	$1,049	$51	$2,248	$51	$2,197
4	$1,100	$1,049	$51	$2,197	$51	$2,146
5	$1,100	$1,049	$51	$2,146	$51	$2,095
46	$1,100	$1,049	$51	$4	$51	$0

Example 2: Mortgage rates have fallen by a *full percentage point.*

$1,100.00 Mortgage Pmt, 8% $2,350.00 Closing Cost, New Mortgage
 -998.00 Mortgage Pmt, 7%   ÷102.00 Monthly Savings
  $102.00 Monthly Savings   24 Months Break Even Point

Month	8% PMT	7% PMT	Monthly Savings	Closing Cost	Monthly Savings	Break Even Point
1	$1,100	$998	$102	$2,350	$102	$2,248
2	$1,100	$998	$102	$2,248	$102	$2,146
3	$1,100	$998	$102	$2,146	$102	$2,044
4	$1,100	$998	$102	$2,044	$102	$1,942
5	$1,100	$998	$102	$1,942	$102	$1,840
24	$1,100	$998	$102	$4	$102	$0

As you see in example one, the break-even point is forty-six months. That means that you would need to stay in your house almost another four years to recoup the closing cost of the new mortgage loan. In the second example, where the interest rate dropped a full percentage point, the break-even point is between twenty-three and twenty-four months. So you would need to remain in your house for only two more years to recoup the closing cost.

Thus, the common belief that you should automatically refinance when mortgage interest rates have dropped by one full percentage point may or may not be true. It requires a little bit of investigation to determine if it is a financially smart decision. To summarize, when mortgage interests rates do drop, and you decide you want to investigate the possibility of refinancing, the first step is to **determine how long you plan to remain in your house.** The next step is to **determine for how long you should refinance the new mortgage loan.**

Refinance and Save Money

Saving money is the second main reason for people choosing to refinance their mortgage loan. Money can be saved in a variety of ways. **One way for people to save money is by *reducing* the term of the mortgage loan** from thirty years to twenty, or perhaps fifteen, or even ten years because mortgage interest rates may have dropped so dramatically as compared to the original interest rate on their present mortgage loan. In this example, let's follow Shawn and Kendra Brown as they go through the steps of trying to save money. When the Browns got their mortgage loan two years ago for $150,000, the interest rate was 9%. The principle and interest mortgage payment at 9% is $1,207.00 per month for thirty years. Looking at an amortization table, the approximate principle mortgage loan balance after twenty-four payments would be approximately $147,800. The total finance charge (or cost) remaining to be paid if the Browns were to keep the 9% mortgage loan for the next twenty-eight years would be $257,680.

Kendra had been watching the news recently and heard that mortgage rates were now down to 7%. That afternoon, Kendra called a couple of mortgage companies and found the consensus to be that it would cost them approximately $2,100.00 in closing cost to refinance. Later that evening after dinner, Shawn and Kendra decide to do some figuring. Kendra says to Shawn, "I heard today that mortgage rates are down to seven percent and I think we should refinance. I called our mortgage company and found out that our current interest rate is nine percent and our principle balance is $147,800." Interested, Shawn goes to the **www.theborrowingmoneyguide.com** website and finds a link to an amortization table. He plugs in some numbers and says to Kendra, "If we were to refinance our current principle loan balance of $147,800 at 7% for 30 years, then our new principle and interest mortgage payment would drop to $983.00 per month and the total finance charge would be $206,200. This would save us $224.00 per month." Kendra then adds, "We could start Junior's college fund and invest the savings."

$1,207.00 Monthly Payment, 9%
 -983.00 Monthly Payment, 7%
 $224.00 Savings per Month, *30 years*

Another benefit is that the Browns would also save $49,380 in finance charges over the life of the loan.

$257,680 Remaining Finance Charge, 9%
-206,200 Total Finance Charge, 7% for *30 years*
   -2,100 Estimated Closing Cost to Refinance
$49,380 Total Savings, *30 years*

Kendra recalls reading Section One of this book (which helped them to buy their first house) that they could potentially **save even more money by** *shortening* **the term of the mortgage loan.** Kendra then proposes this question to Shawn, "What if we were to refinance our mortgage loan at 7% but reduce the term of the mortgage loan to either twenty or fifteen years?" Looking at the amortization table, Shawn determines the mortgage loan payment would be $1,145.00 for a twenty-year loan and $1,328.00 for a fifteen-year loan. Kendra and Shawn then talk about their family budget. They agree that their family budget can support a slight increase in their mortgage payment with a fifteen-year loan, but the payment will make things a little tight. Kendra looks at the amortization table and sees that the total finance charge (or cost) of the fifteen-year loan at 7% is only $91,300. Therefore, the fifteen-year mortgage loan will save the Browns an incredible $164,280 in finance charges over the life of the loan! Kendra says to Shawn, "Since Junior is only three years old, the house will be paid for by the time he is ready for college. We will be able to use the equity in our house to help pay for his college."

$257,680 Remaining Finance Charge, 9%
 -91,300 Total Finance Charge, 7% for *15 years*
   -2,100 Estimated Closing Cost to Refinance
$164,280 Total Savings, *15 years*

But Shawn is a little curious about the possibility of saving money monthly *and* over the life of the loan. So Shawn decides to look at a twenty-year loan term. With another baby on the way, Shawn thinks that a fifteen-year term would be too much of a strain on their monthly family budget. Looking at the amortization table again,

Shawn sees that the total finance charge (or cost) of the twenty-year loan at 7% is $127,300. So for the twenty-year mortgage loan, the cost savings over the life of the loan would be $128,380. Shawn informs Kendra, "The twenty-year loan will still give us a significant amount of cost savings and our house will almost be paid for by the time Junior starts college. But, the best part is that the new loan will save us $62.00 per month, which will be enough to pay for the extra groceries and diapers for the new baby."

$257,680 Remaining Finance Charge, 9%
-127,200 Total Finance Charge, 7% for *20 years*
-2,100 Estimated Closing Cost to Refinance
$128,380 Total Savings, *20 years*

$1,207.00 Monthly Payment, 9%
-1,145.00 Monthly Payment, 7%
$62.00 Savings per Month, *20 years*

Refinance and Consolidate Debt

Another way for people to save money through refinancing a mortgage loan is by consolidating consumer debt. **If you have accumulated equity in your house, or your house has substantially appreciated in value, then you can use that equity in your house as an income producing asset.** You could possibly increase your income by fifteen percent or more by making your house "work" for you instead of you always working for your house. This is called a "cash out" refinance.

Typically, mortgage loans have the lowest interest rate and the longest repayment term available as compared to consumer loans, especially so after you factor in the potential tax savings. Currently, mortgage interest is the only type of interest consumers pay that is tax deductible (please consult your tax advisor). Consumer loans, which are discussed in Section Four, such as credit cards, student loans (some student loan interest is now tax deductible, but with restrictions), car loans, and personal lines of credit generally have higher overall interest rates than first mortgage loans.   By consolidating your consumer loans into a first mortgage refinance, you can save hundreds or even thousands of dollars each month in total monthly payments.   That could be the equivalent of getting a fifteen-percent raise! And when was the last time your employer gave you that kind of raise?

In this example, let's follow along with Andrew and Maya Carter as they figure out how to get out of debt and save money.   The Carters have been getting deeper into debt over the last couple of years.   Their current monthly principle and interest mortgage payment is $1,000.00.   The current principle balance on their mortgage loan is $150,000.   The Carters now pay over $700.00 a month in credit card payments on $30,000 of total credit card debt.   Both Andrew and Maya each recently needed a new car so they financed a total of $40,000.   The combined car payment for the two new automobiles amounts to $650.00 per month.   Over the summer, their oldest daughter got married so they took out a $5,000.00 personal loan that has a $200.00 monthly payment.   The Carters are now paying a total of $2,550.00 per month separately for these debts (loans).

$1,000.00 Mortgage Payment	$150,000 Mortgage Loan Balance
+700.00 Credit Card Pmt.	+30,000 Credit Card Debt
+650.00 Auto Loan Pmt.	+40,000 Auto Loan Balances
+200.00 Personal Loan Pmt.	+5,000 Personal Loan Balance
$2,550.00 Total Monthly Debt	$225,000 Total Amount Owed

Andrew has read the beginning part of Section Two in this book. He has discussed with Maya their situation and agreed that this is the house in which they plan to retire, so it makes good financial sense to refinance for thirty years.   Maya tells Andrew that she just found out this week that the factory where she presently works is being closed and that she will be receiving three months worth of severance pay. She tells her husband, "I would love to retire and not have to worry about looking for another job so I can watch our grandkids, but I don't think we can afford our current obligations and enjoy our same lifestyle with just your income."

Andrew knows that they need to reduce their debts in order to keep their credit in good standing and also to take the pressure off of his wife about finding another job. Andrew also knows that his house has appreciated in value and is now worth $285,000. Andrew says to Maya," I think we have enough equity in our house to refinance all of our consumer debt into one large loan." Andrews does some figuring and determines that they have $228,000 of available equity using 80% of the value of their home.

$285,000 Market Value of Home
x   80% Standard Loan-to-value Threshold
$228,000 Available Equity

Andrew now knows that they have enough equity in their house to consolidate all of their loans. He goes to the amortization table and finds that a new thirty-year mortgage loan for $225,000, which will pay off all their debts, at 7% would yield a new monthly principle and interest mortgage payment of only $1,496.00 per month. He excitedly turns to Maya and says," That is a monthly savings of $1,054.00 per month, enough to allow you to retire!"

$2,550.00 Total Monthly Debts
-1,496.00 New Mortgage Loan Payment
$1,054.00 Savings per Month

Suppose Mr. Carter's annual income is $75,000 per year, which equals $6,250.00 per month before taxes and other deductions. With the consolidation loan, the Carters now have an extra $1,054.00 of cash in their pockets each month. The

$1,054 per month in savings equates to a 16.9% raise in their household income because the Carters made the equity in their house work for them!

$1,054.00 Savings per Month
÷6,250.00 Gross Monthly Income
16.90%   Raise

Chapter 2: Getting Your Financial Affairs in Order

Great! You have now determined whether or not you want to refinance. If you have determined that you do, the next thing is to get your financial affairs in order. If you are pretty sure that you have established good credit and pay your bills on time, then you may be tempted to skip ahead to the next chapter. But don't fool yourself, you might have some credit blemishes or some "slow pay" history in your credit file that you may not be aware of. It is also possible that there could be some erroneously reported delinquencies in your credit file. For these reasons, it is advisable that you continue reading. These credit blemishes or "slow pay" histories will be uncovered by the mortgage loan officer or underwriter and analyzing them could slow the application process or cause your loan to be declined.

You will go through the same basic process of qualifying for a mortgage loan as when you purchased your home (as discussed in Section One) but the overall process is a little more streamlined. **I recommend that you do not make any major purchases on credit or open any new consumer loans until you have closed this new mortgage loan.** Opening any new credit cards or consumer loans could adversely affect your debt-to-income ratio and potentially cause your mortgage loan to be declined. (The debt-to-income ratio will be discussed in Chapter Three.) It could also adversely affect your credit score thereby not allowing you to qualify for the best interest rates.

If you have not reviewed your credit report in over a year, it is advisable to review it now. If your credit is *not* in good shape, than you might not be able to refinance your loan and take advantage of lowering your interest rate or saving money. You can request a copy of your credit file by contacting one of the three major credit bureau reporting agencies (Equifax, Experian or TransUnion) listed at the end of Section Six, Chapter Four. The credit report should cost you less than fifteen dollars, but it is well worth it. A few states have a law that allows you to request and review a copy of your credit file free of charge at least once a year.

When you receive your credit file, check the report closely for any discrepancies or errors. If there are any errors or delinquencies that you do not agree with, you will be able to dispute those references and accounts through the credit bureau agency from which you ordered the report. Along with the credit report package will be a form and information on how to go about disputing any data contained in the report. Another way to dispute the credit reference is to contact the creditor directly. **If you have contacted the creditor directly and a representative has agreed to correct the error, make sure that you get the correction in *writing*.** I have seen many situations in which a borrower will state on a loan application that a collection has been paid off or that a late payment error has been corrected, but comes to find out that the creditor has not reported the correct information to any credit bureau. Other times, the information might only get reported to one of the credit bureau agencies, but not the primary one being used for this loan. This could either cause a delay in the verification process, cause the loan to be declined, or cause the credit reference to remain against you. Having the credit reference remain counting against you could result in a lower credit grade for you and potentially force you to pay a higher interest rate. **As a rule, you should keep any correspondence, including written corrected account information, for at least the next five to seven years.**

If you have any current delinquencies, you need to pay them. **The better your credit is, the better the interest rate, and the more equity in your house you will be able to use.** The reason for this is that the higher your credit score is, based on statistical models, the less likely it will be that you will default or become late with your mortgage payment. Therefore, your mortgage loan will cost less to service and the savings are passed on to you in the form of a lower interest rate. Typically, anyone with a credit score in the range of 620 to 650 or higher, with reasonably good overall credit, who does not have a bankruptcy on record within the last seven years, and does not have any unpaid judgments or collections will be able to get the preferred mortgage interest rates.

If you have filed a bankruptcy in the last ten years, you should get your bankruptcy paperwork together, including the discharge papers. You might not need them if your bankruptcy was discharged over five years ago, but it is best to be prepared so that if they are required, the loan process will not be delayed. Another reason you may need your bankruptcy discharge paperwork is that perhaps not all of the credit that was included in the bankruptcy was reported properly. Some creditors might continue to show an account as delinquent, indicating that you still owe them money, or as if they charged your account off when, in fact, it was discharged in the bankruptcy and you are no longer responsible for that particular debt. By having your bankruptcy discharge paperwork readily available, you will be able to prove what debts were actually a part of the bankruptcy filing. In addition, be prepared to discuss and provide a written explanation as to why you filed a bankruptcy in the first place or why you have had any late payments.

To summarize how to get your financial affairs in order:
- Order a copy of your credit file from one of the three main credit reporting agencies.

- Ensure that all of the information being reported is accurate. Make corrections if needed and remember to get the corrections in writing.
- If you have any current delinquencies, you need to pay them.
- If you filed a bankruptcy within the last ten years, then have your bankruptcy discharge papers available.

Chapter 3: Documenting Your Income

Being able to verify your income is the next step in the mortgage loan process. **You will need to be able to prove how much income you make on a *regular and consistent basis*.** If you are an hourly or salary employee, you will need to have your last two paychecks and the last two years of your W-2 Wage and Tax Statements on hand. If you are an hourly employee and receive any overtime, you will need to be able to prove that the income has been consistent over the last two or more years. Most lenders will not include additional income if it is only seasonal or inconsistent. If you are a salary employee who consistently receives a regular quarterly or yearly bonus, you will need to prove that you receive that extra income on a consistent basis as well. When verifying your income, most lenders or underwriters will look at the year-to-date gross income from your most recent paycheck and then average it with either the last year or two of your W-2 Wage and Tax Statements. **However, it is not a good idea to use overtime or bonus income to qualify for a loan.** When the overtime is stopped or the bonus income is gone, you might not be able to afford your present debt load or your current standard of living. This could have a damaging effect on your credit rating and the credit score that you worked so hard to build. It is also not a good idea to base your family budget on this extra income.

If you are a "commission only" salesperson, you will need to be able to prove your income in the same manner as the salary employee does. **With commission income, an underwriter is looking for what your *average income* has been over the last two or more years, not what your best month or quarter has been.** If you have just started a new job and will be paid primarily by commissions or large bonuses, then it would be best to conservatively estimate the income that you will be claiming on the mortgage loan application. If you have just changed professions and started a new job as a commission only employee (i.e., going from a school teacher to a commission real estate agent), then you may have to postpone refinancing your first mortgage loan until your income has stabilized and you have been on the job for at least twelve months. In any event, it is always best to apply for a mortgage loan and let the mortgage company review your income situation.

Being self-employed is sometimes a more complicated situation when it comes to verifying your income. One reason is because self-employed people generally fall into two categories based on the way they report their income on their federal tax returns. They can either report the true income (sales) from their business, with the proper deductions and expenses, and pay the proper federal and state income taxes or they can not report the true income, inflate the deductibles and expenses as much as possible, thereby greatly reducing their tax obligations. **As a self-employed borrower, you will qualify for a mortgage loan a lot easier if an underwriter can use your adjusted gross income listed at the bottom of the first page of your 1040 Federal Income Tax Returns.** In some cases, the underwriter will be able to add back to your adjusted gross income any depreciation or interest expense you may have claimed. Depending on the type of business structure you have (Sole Proprietor, Limited Liability Company, or "S" Corporation, to name a few) and if you are attempting to qualify for a conventional mortgage loan, will determine how your federal income tax returns are interpreted. Each lender has an internal analysis on how they review self-employment income and business debt. To reiterate, as a self-employed borrower, you will qualify for the best rates if an underwriter can use the income directly from your federal tax returns with little or no manipulations or adjustments. Therefore, you should have on hand the last two years of your federal tax returns with all schedules along with the last couple of months of business bank statements, in case they are required.

If you "hide" your income in order to avoid paying federal income taxes, then you might have to use an alternative method to prove your income and you might have to search for a non-traditional or unconventional mortgage lender. There are lenders who offer special loan programs that do not require any proof of income, commonly known as "no-doc" loans, or have flexible income requirements. These types of loans come with higher interest rates and generally have higher fees and closing costs than a conventional mortgage loan. Typically, when attempting to qualify for these alternative types of loans, you will need some combination of federal tax returns, bank statements, a financial statement, and a Profit and Loss Statement for your company.

The purpose of the Profit and Loss Statement is to show the mortgage company how your business is performing over the last quarter or last twelve months. To support the gross income, or sales, that you have claimed for the current year on the Profit and Loss Statement, you will need to have your last six to twelve months of business bank statements on hand. The reason the bank statements are important is that they act as your pay stub. Typically, when you receive money from a customer for goods purchased or services rendered, you deposit the money into a particular business checking account, similar to a wage earner depositing his regular weekly paycheck. Then the bills are paid from that business checking account. For this reason, it is

recommended that you keep separate checking or deposit accounts for your business
and your personal use.

An example of a simple Profit and Loss Statement looks like this:

ABC Company
1/1/04 through 8/30/04

Gross Receipts or Sales		$200,000
Cost of Goods Sold (materials)		($85,000)
Gross Profit		$115,000
Expenses		
Wages & Salaries	$40,000	
Automotive Expenses	$15,000	
Other Expenses	$10,000	
Total Expenses		($65,000)
Net Income		$50,000

By law, you do not have to disclose whether you receive any child support or
alimony payments unless you need that additional income to qualify because of your
debt-to-income ratio. If you do receive child support or alimony from an ex-spouse
and you plan on claiming that income in your mortgage application, you will need to
be able to prove that you receive the support payments on a *regular* and *consistent*
basis. You can make a copy of the last couple of support checks you have received
or you can get your last six to twelve months of bank statements together that shows
the support income as being consistently received. It is also a good idea to get
copies of the court ordered child support paperwork, or the signed and recorded
divorce decree, to add additional support to the income you are claiming. However,
you might not be able to use child support income if the dependent will be reaching
adult status, typically eighteen years of age, in the near future. Also, alimony
income might not be able to be used if the income has certain restrictions such as
getting remarried or a termination date that is in the near future.

If you are on a fixed income or you receive a subsidized income (i.e., social security, disability, workman's compensation, or retirement income, to name a few), then you will need to be able to prove how much money you receive on a *monthly* and *consistent* basis and how long you will be receiving it. You will need to get your last year's 1099 Federal Wage Form and the most recent Award Letter or monthly check stub together. If you have direct deposit for this money, then you can use the last two months of your bank statements. Depending on the type of income you receive, you might also have to get a letter from your employer, or from the source of that income, stating how long this income is expected to continue.

By law, you cannot be discriminated against for the type of income you receive. **The key is being able to verify that whatever income you are receiving and using to qualify for the mortgage loan, will be consistently received by you on a regular and ongoing basis.** You should never let your income discourage you from applying for a loan. It is always best to apply for the loan, provide proof of your income, and let the mortgage company determine how much income is verifiable and can be used with your loan application.

The Debt-to-Income Ratio

After you have gathered the documents proving your income, you can calculate your own debt-to-income ratio. How to do that will be explained shortly. To understand the guidelines, **your debt-to-income ratio should be at forty percent or less in order to qualify for the best interest rates offered.** Most mortgage companies' debt-to-income ratio underwriting guidelines typically fall between thirty-six and forty percent. However, there are companies that will lend money to people with higher debt-to-income ratios, some up to fifty percent, or on a rare occasion, to sixty percent. The drawback of having a higher debt-to-income ratio means that these companies will charge a substantially higher interest rate and it will generally cost you more in terms of closing costs and fees than if your ratio was under forty.

The purpose of the debt-to-income ratio is to determine if you can afford to repay the new mortgage loan payment, in addition to continuing paying your other remaining debts, based on the underwriter's assessment. The debt-to-income ratio is calculated by adding up your total monthly debts (creditors only, no utility bills), adding in the proposed new mortgage payment, and then dividing that number by your verified gross monthly income.

Example:

$1,300.00	New Mortgage	$3,000	Your Income
Do not include	Cell Phone	+2,000	Spouses Income
Do not include	Auto Ins.	$5,000	Total Family Income
Do not include	Electric Bill		
$50.00	Credit Card Pmt.	$1,775	Total Mo. Debts
$100.00	Credit Card Pmt.	÷5,000	Total Family Income
$325.00	Car Loan	**35.5%**	**Debt-to-Income Ratio**
$1,775.00	Total Mo. Debts		

As you can see in this example, you do not include utility bills (such as electric bill, insurance bill, cable bill, or phone bill) in the calculation. For your charge cards or lines of credit, a good rule of thumb is to use three percent of your current principle balance as a monthly payment when figuring the debt-to-income ratio. For your personal or installment loans, you will use the regular monthly payment. So, based on the example given, this couple has a debt-to-income ratio of 36% and would qualify for the mortgage loan. However, even if the mortgage company says you qualify for the loan, make sure you are comfortable with the mortgage payment and that the monthly payment, **including the escrow payment,** fits into *your* family budget.

To summarize documenting your income:

- For an hourly or salary employee, you will need a copy of your last two paychecks and last two years of your W-2 Wage and Tax Statement.

- For a commission salesperson, you will need a copy of your last two paychecks and last two years of your W-2 Wage and Tax Statement.

- For a self-employed person, qualifying for a conventional mortgage loan, you should have the last two years of your federal tax returns with all schedules along with the last couple of months of business bank statements, in case they are required.

- For a self-employed person, qualifying for a non-traditional or alternative loan program, you should have the last two years of your federal tax returns with all schedules along with a Profit and Loss Statement, a financial statement, and the last six to twelve months of business bank statements.

- For an individual using child support or alimony income, you will need a copy of the section from the divorce decree which outlines the support payments, a copy of the last two support checks, and the last six months of your bank statements.

- For an individual who receives a fixed or subsidized income, you will need a copy of the most recent Award Letter, the last year of the 1099 Federal Wage and Tax Form, the last two months of your bank statements, and the last two years of your federal tax returns.

Chapter 4: What Type of Mortgage Loan Do I Need?

You have now decided that it makes good financial sense to refinance. To help you choose the correct mortgage loan product that fits your current need, you need to answer a few questions:

- Do you want a fixed interest rate or are you comfortable with a variable or adjustable rate?
- Do you want to have the real estate taxes and homeowner's insurance escrowed (included in) with the mortgage payment?
- Do you want to avoid paying mortgage insurance (generally required on conventional mortgage loans when you exceed eighty percent loan-to-value, mortgage insurance and loan-to-value are discussed in Chapter Five)?
- How long is it until you retire?
- Do you want extra cash in your pocket if there is any equity available?

Your mortgage loan officer needs to know the answers to the questions listed above in order to fully understand what your long-term goals and short-term plans are. That way the loan officer will be able to give you his or her recommendation for what type of loan product you should get as well as what different terms are available.

Shown below are the six different types of mortgage programs available with brief summaries describing each one and its main benefits. Your mortgage loan officer can help you to understand each type of loan in greater detail if you need further clarification.

Loan Option One: The Fixed Rate Mortgage Loan

The Fixed Rate Mortgage Loan is the most popular and widely granted mortgage loan. It is the most simple to understand and is most likely the type of loan you got if you have already bought and financed a first home. The monthly principle and interest payment and the interest rate are fixed for the entire loan. That means that they will not change for the life of the loan as long as the loan is being repaid as agreed. The length (or term) of the loan is generally 10, 15, 20, 25 or 30 years. The most frequently used loan term is the thirty-year loan, followed by the fifteen-year loan. (The examples discussed in Chapter Two were based on the Fixed Rate Mortgage Loan product.)

The benefits of this loan are that:

- It is the most basic type of mortgage loan and the easiest to understand.
- The terms are fixed for the duration of the loan.

If you have a lot of equity in your home and a lot of consumer debt, you can consolidate all your debts into one loan, saving you money each month. By consolidating consumer debt when you refinance, you can increase your tax deductions because the interest paid on any mortgage loan, up to the market value of the home, is potentially tax deductible.

Loan Option Two: The ARM (Adjustable Rate Mortgage) Loan

The ARM Loan starts out as a Fixed Rate Mortgage Loan and then turns into a variable (adjustable) interest rate loan after the fixed rate period has expired. This loan will allow you to get an interest rate that is initially lower than the Fixed Rate Mortgage Loan because the fixed rate time period of the ARM loan is a much shorter term. The fixed rate period is usually for one, three, five or seven years. The three and five year terms are the most widely used. **A key to remember is that the *shorter* the fixed rate period of the ARM loan, the lower the initial interest rate will be.** The fixed rate period means that the monthly principle and interest payment and the interest rate will remain the same during this period of time, just like the Fixed Rate Mortgage Loan. After the fixed period of time expires, the loan then becomes a variable interest rate loan. The monthly principle and interest payment will change according to how high or low the new variable interest rate becomes. Over time, the interest rate will increase to the current market interest rate, which could be higher than the Fixed Rate Mortgage Loan that was offered to you when you originally applied.

If you plan to keep the mortgage loan when it enters the adjustment period, then **you will want to make sure that you can afford the monthly payment if the interest rate hits the preset rate ceiling.** The preset rate ceiling is the highest interest rate that you could be charged for the loan during the adjustment period. This rate will be listed on the loan contract (promissory note). You also need to find out how often the interest rate will adjust in the "adjustable" period. Some ARM Loans will adjust monthly, but most will adjust once a year. If your loan does adjust once a year, you will need to know what the maximum rate adjustment is for each year. Most ARM loans will only be able to adjust up or down one or two percentage points at a time. The key to success for the ARM loan is to sell the house, or refinance the mortgage loan prior to, or shortly after, the adjustment period starts.

Use this loan when:

- You are buying a house that is a little more than what you can easily afford now, but you anticipate an increase in your family's income before the adjustment period starts.
- You plan on selling the property in a couple of years and want to take advantage of a lower monthly payment and a lower interest rate (initially) than the Fixed Rate Mortgage Loan.
- You can save money in finance charges (interest payments) in the short term with an ARM Loan when compared to a Fixed Rate Mortgage Loan because of the lower initial interest rate.

Loan Option Three: The Balloon Loan

The Balloon Loan is similar to the ARM Loan, but with two main differences. The first difference concerns when the fixed interest rate period of the loan ends. While the ARM Loan is usually fixed for three to five years, the balloon loan typically has a fixed interest rate for a longer time period, usually for five, ten or fifteen years. The second difference is that when the initial fixed interest rate period of the balloon ends, the whole principle balance becomes due and payable, unlike the ARM Loan which turns into an adjustable rate mortgage loan. Under the Balloon Loan, this "due and payable" feature is known as the "call" feature. When the Balloon Loan note matures, the remaining principle balance and any unpaid interest must be repaid to the bank or lending company. To satisfy the debt, you could payoff the loan in cash, refinance the loan balance into a whole new loan, or sell the property. A similarity of the Balloon Loan to the previous two loans mentioned is that the monthly principle and interest payment can be based on (or amortized as) a thirty-year loan.

Use this loan when:

- You plan on keeping the mortgage loan for a longer period of time than the ARM Loan can provide under the *fixed* interest rate period.
- You can get a slightly lower interest rate than the Fixed Rate Mortgage Loan.
- You can get a low monthly principle and interest payment based on a twenty or thirty year (amortization period) loan term.

Loan Option Four: The Line of Credit Loan

The Line of Credit Loan generally appeals to people who have paid off, or owe very little on, their home and want access to money by getting a (potentially) tax deductible Line of Credit Loan. As a *first* mortgage, the Line of Credit Loan is generally for people with high monthly incomes who want the convenience of having access to thousands of dollars in cash without having to liquidate investments. The Line of Credit Loan helps the borrower to make large purchases such as buying a new car, buying investment property, doing major home improvement work, or purchasing stock. The repayment of the borrowed funds (money) is supposed to be done in a short period of time. Therefore, the person who gets this type of mortgage loan can afford to pay large monthly principle payments.

For most people with an income between thirty and seventy-five thousand dollars per year, the Line of Credit Loan is usually done as a *second* mortgage loan with a credit line of ten to fifty thousand dollars. This type of Home Equity Loan is discussed further in Section Three, Chapter Four.

There are three main differences between the Line of Credit Loan and the Fixed Rate Mortgage Loan. The first difference is that the interest rate for a First Mortgage Line of Credit Loan will initially be lower than the interest rate for the Fixed Rate Mortgage Loan because the interest rate is a pure variable rate loan. The interest rate will go up or down whenever the index rate that the loan is tied to changes. The index rate is usually the U.S. prime rate or the LIBOR (London Interbank Offered Rate) rate. If mortgage interest rates increase over time, then the interest rate attached to the Line of Credit Loan could end up becoming a much higher interest rate than the original fixed interest rate that was offered with the Fixed Rate Mortgage Loan. The second difference is that the minimum monthly payment will change every month because the monthly payment is generally based on the average loan balance from the previous month, similar to a credit card. The third difference is that, of the four mortgage products already mentioned, the Line of Credit Loan can have the lowest monthly payment option. **The key to success with the Line of Credit Loan is that if you have a large line of credit, and you were to use it all, that you could easily afford to make the minimum monthly payment at its highest interest rate level.**

This loan would be attractive if:

- You need to have access to cash in the near future for large purchases or expenses (i.e., major renovations, to purchase a car, college tuition, etc.).
- You do not want to liquidate investments that would be subject to capital gain taxes.
- You need easy access to cash with potentially tax deductible interest.
- You don't want to spend time and money applying for another loan because after you pay off the loan balance, the line of credit remains open for future use.
- You want a loan that has the lowest minimum monthly payment option of the four loans mentioned.

Loan Option Five: The Reverse Mortgage Loan

The Reverse Mortgage Loan primarily benefits people who have a house that is paid for (or owe very little on) and need additional monthly income to supplement their fixed income. Generally, retired people over sixty two years of age benefit from a Reverse Mortgage. Once approved for this type of loan, instead of getting all of the money up front, the borrowed money comes in equal monthly installments. This type of loan is used to supplement your current monthly income. The borrower would receive a predetermined check each month until the loan reaches maturity, typically thirty years, or until all borrowers pass away. A Reverse Mortgage Loan would be a good loan for someone who may not have many investments, has little or no retirement income other than social security, but has a very substantial amount of equity in his or her house.

A key consideration for this loan is that you will need to make plans for what to do when the loan reaches maturity. When it reaches maturity, not only will the monthly checks stop coming, but the loan will have to be repaid. A second Reverse Mortgage Loan will not be an option since you will now owe a substantial amount of money against your house. The house will either have to be sold or you will have to get a traditional mortgage loan and start repaying back the money owed (but you would not have the extra income source to help repay the loan). It would be wise to talk to your children (or heirs to the estate) about this loan, especially if they are looking to inherit the property, and discuss the possibility of what will happen if you outlive the maturity date or pass away during the loan payment period of the Reverse Mortgage Loan.

Why this loan is attractive:
- The loan supplements your monthly retirement income.
- It allows you to use your home as an investment tool whereby you receive a guaranteed monthly income stream for up to thirty years.

Loan Option Six: The Negative Amortization Loan

The Negative Amortization Loan is only suitable for people who are in a very "hot" housing market in which properties are appreciating at a substantial rate; increasing ten to twenty percent or more in value per year. This is important because the principle mortgage balance of the loan will not decrease over time. The easiest way to explain the negative amortization loan is to look at an example. Let's say you originally got a $300,000 mortgage loan at the current market interest rate of 8%. The monthly principle and interest payment, looking at an amortization table, would be $2,201.00. Under the Negative Amortization Loan, the monthly mortgage payment is calculated from a lesser predetermined interest rate of, say, 5%. Looking at the amortization table again, that would make the monthly principle and interest payment $1,610.00. The difference between the two payments is added back to the loan balance. That will cause the principle balance of your loan to increase over time. After the first monthly payment was made on the loan, the loan balance would have increased to $300,591. When it comes time to sell your home or to refinance, you will owe more money than what you originally borrowed.

There are two disadvantages to this type of loan. One is that you will most likely not be able to get a second mortgage. The second disadvantage is that if the housing market cools off and the property value of homes drops considerably, you could wind up owing more money on the mortgage loan than what your house would then be worth.

Why this loan would be worthwhile:

- Your principle and interest monthly payment is a lot less than it would be when compared to a conventional mortgage loan.
- It allows you to buy a home in a very appealing, very expensive market that you would otherwise not be able to afford.
- Your home will appreciate in value a lot more than homes in slower markets, thus earning you more money on your investment in the long run.

Chapter 5: Tips and Pointers

Tip 1: The benefits of a short-term loan

If you are getting a fixed rate mortgage loan, **the shorter the mortgage term the more money you will save in finance charges** (interest cost). This can be very substantial over the life of the loan. Ask your lender for a Preliminary Truth in Lending Disclosure for a fifteen-year and a thirty-year mortgage loan. Compare the monthly payment, the total finance charge (cost of the loan) and the total payback. If you can't afford the monthly payment for the fifteen-year loan, then look at getting a twenty or twenty-five year mortgage loan.

Tip 2: Pay extra principle payments whenever possible

A great way to save lots of money over the life of your mortgage loan is to always pay an extra principle amount. The resulting savings over the life of the loan by doing this can be very substantial. Consider this, for a thirty-year $150,000 mortgage loan, paying extra principle could reduce the length of the loan by five or more years and would save you well over $50,000 in finance charges!

There are several ways to pay extra principle. The first way is to pay an extra amount, whether its ten dollars or two hundred dollars, with each mortgage payment...whatever you can afford based on your monthly family budget. A second way is to pay a thirteenth payment at the end of each calendar year. A third way to save money in total finance charges is to pay half of your mortgage payment every two weeks, which will also equal thirteen annualized payments.

If you choose the second or third way to pay extra principle, then you need to verify the repayment plan with the mortgage company to make sure the extra payment is allowed. **The key to saving money by paying extra principle is that you must be consistent and always note on the monthly statement or payment coupon that the extra amount is to be applied to the** *principle balance.* If you don't tell the mortgage company where you want the extra money to go, then they will probably place the extra money in your escrow account.

The best part of paying extra principle is that you are not contractually obligated to pay extra money every month. It is simply your choice based on your ability to pay. Any time you can send extra money to reduce the principle balance, the greater your savings will be over the life of the loan.

Tip 3: Paying off consumer debt

If you have refinanced and gotten a new mortgage loan to pay off credit card debt, or other consumer loans, then you should not use those lines of credit again once they are paid off. **When you are consolidating debt, the key is to save money by** *eliminating* **the other debt and having only one monthly payment.** If you do decide to reuse those charge cards and incur significant debt, you will be in worse financial trouble. In addition, **you will not have the equity in your house to solve the new financial problem.** More than likely, you will not be able to refinance the mortgage loan again for a couple of years until equity has been built up in your house again.

If you are paying off consumer debt with a new mortgage loan, it is also important that you **CONTINUE** to pay the regular monthly payment on these loans until you actually close your new mortgage loan. **Even if the loan officer tells you**

otherwise. There is always the possibility that the new loan could be delayed, that a payoff check could get mailed to a wrong address, or that a payoff check could be applied to a wrong account by the creditor. If any of this happens, and you have *not* continued to pay your regular monthly payment, the debt could get reported to the credit bureau as being delinquent. This would cause your credit score to drop and possibly cause you future problems with qualifying for loans.

Tip 4: Continue to escrow for taxes and insurance

Most people should continue to escrow for their homeowner's insurance and real estate taxes when they refinance unless they have enough discipline to put away money each month into a savings account in order to pay for these two important bills when they become due. In almost all cases, the mortgage company will *not* charge you a fee for this service. It is also very convenient to have these bills paid by the mortgage company. However, if the mortgage company fails to pay these bills when due, you are still liable for the payments (but this is a very rare exception and not the norm).

Homeowner's insurance is a requirement of the mortgage company because it protects your home, which is probably your largest asset, and which actually is the mortgage company's collateral. If you let your homeowner's insurance coverage expire, the mortgage company has the right to place their own fire protection insurance coverage on your house, but this coverage will only protect the mortgage company's loss and *none of your assets*. The mortgage company will also charge your loan an annual premium that is typically much higher than the standard homeowner's policy.

The real estate tax must be paid when due because it is one of the major funding sources of your local government. If you fail to pay your taxes in a timely manner on your property, the county or state has the right to place a lien on your property for the amount owed and could eventually force the property to be sold at a foreclosure sale.

Tip 5: Avoid paying mortgage insurance

Another type of cost that could be added to the monthly escrow payment is mortgage insurance, also known as PMI or private mortgage insurance. Mortgage insurance is an insurance policy that protects the mortgage company from any loss they might incur (should you default on your mortgage loan) because they agreed to lend you more than eighty percent of the value of your home *and* you are getting a "conventional" mortgage loan. (A "conventional" mortgage loan is a mortgage loan where the bank or mortgage broker, after closing your loan, sells the loan and possibly it's servicing rights to another bank or financial institution on the secondary market. If the servicing rights to your loan are sold, then you would make your regular monthly payment to another company.) However, because of this insurance, mortgage companies are able to lend borrowers up to, in some cases, one hundred percent of the value of their home thus making home ownership possible for a lot of people who might not qualify otherwise.

PMI can be expensive, but it can often be avoided. The two reasons people choose to avoid this insurance product are: (1) The money paid towards this monthly insurance premium is *not* tax deductible and (2) the benefit is paid to the mortgage company. If you want to avoid paying a mortgage insurance premium, you can opt for a first mortgage/second mortgage combination loan (also known as an "80/10", "80/15"or "80/20" loan). That way, the interest you pay on the second mortgage loan is typically tax deductible as opposed to the mortgage insurance monthly premium expense that is not. The combination loan means that the first mortgage loan would be for the loan amount equal to eighty percent ("80") of the value of the home. The second number represents what the second mortgage loan balance would be as a percentage of the value of the home, either ten percent ("10"), fifteen percent ("15"), or twenty percent ("20").

Mortgage insurance, or PMI, works this way. For this example, assume that your house is worth $150,000 and you need to borrow $135,000. That makes the loan-to-value ratio 90%.

$135,000 Loan Amount
÷ $150,000 Market Value of Home
_____
90%   Loan-to-Value

The mortgage insurance premium (because you are financing more than eighty percent of the value of the home) will cost $.65 per $1,000 of the property value for this example. That equates to an extra $87.75 per month added to your total monthly mortgage payment.

$135,000 Loan Balance $135.00
÷1,000 Of Value   x $.65 PMI Value
_____   _____
$135.00 $87.75 Per Month added to Escrow

To avoid paying mortgage insurance, you would get a first mortgage/second mortgage combination loan. In this case it would be called an "80/10" loan because you need to borrow up to 90% of the value of the home (80%+10%= 90%). The first mortgage loan balance would be $120,000 and the second mortgage loan would be for $15,000.

$150,000	Value of Home		$150,000	Value of Home
x 80%	Loan-to-value		x 10%	Loan-to-value
$120,000	First Mortgage Loan		$15,000	Second Mortgage Loan

Remember to check with your first mortgage lender to see if they have any restrictions on getting a second mortgage. In some cases the combined monthly payment could be a little higher than the one mortgage payment, so make sure that the two payments fit in your family budget.

Tip 6: Avoid prepayment penalties

Make sure to ask the lending company if your new mortgage loan will have a prepayment penalty or not. A prepayment penalty is a fee paid to the lender for the privilege of paying off a loan prior to maturity to compensate the lender for loss of future income on the loan. Most prepayment terms are usually for three or five years. If you plan on having the loan longer than the prepayment penalty period, then having one will not matter. If at all possible though, **I would recommend that you find a loan that does not have a prepayment penalty.** If you plan on selling your home in the near future and you have a prepayment penalty, check the language to make sure the penalty is waived when you sell the property. Prepayment penalties are now illegal in some states. Again, check with your lender.

Tip 7: Always find out how much the loan will cost

Always find out how many origination (prepaid) points your loan has attached to it. An origination (prepaid) point, commonly known as an origination fee, is money paid to the lender as a fee for service. One origination point equals one percent of the mortgage loan balance. Most loans come with one to three origination points. This fee is generally tax deductible. You can also sometimes "buy down" your interest rate by paying an additional origination point or two, called a "discount point". It might be worthwhile to "buy down" the interest rate if you plan to keep the mortgage for a long period of time because a lower interest rate over the life of the loan will save you a lot more money than what the discount fee cost.

Find out from the lender if there are any out-of-pocket closing costs you have to pay or if they are included in the loan. This is especially important if you do not have any money in savings or would prefer to just keep your cash. Most loan programs allow you to add (or roll) the closing cost into the loan. As a reminder, financing the closing cost in with the loan means you will be paying interest on these added costs.

Tip 8: Never pay any money up-front to a Mortgage Broker

<u>Never</u> pay any money when completing a loan application to a mortgage broker in order to retain his/her service for a mortgage loan. The only costs you might have to pay when applying for the loan are the appraisal fee on your home and ordering a credit report. These two costs combined should be no more than three hundred to four hundred dollars. The credit report alone should cost no more than fifty dollars. However, do not pay for these services until you have reviewed the pre-disclosure package, which will be discussed in the next chapter, *and* **until you have decided to go through this particular mortgage broker for your loan.** If you decide to use a mortgage broker, he or she should not get compensated (paid) until your loan has *closed*.

Chapter 6: Applying for the Loan

The first step in the loan approval process is to find a mortgage company and a loan officer. To find a mortgage company, you will need to do some research. You should get at least two or three rate quotes. One place to check mortgage interest rates is at a lender's web site. Another option is to contact the mortgage loan officer affiliated with your local bank. In addition, you could check with the business section of your local newspaper. You will want to compare the mortgage interest rates, prepaid points (commonly known as origination fees) and closing costs (such as processing fee, attorney fee, application fee, document preparation fee, and appraisal fee to name a few). Choose the mortgage loan officer or lender with whom you are most comfortable with and/or gives you the best overall deal.

Sometimes the lender who offers you the lowest interest rate may not be offering the best overall *value*. A mortgage company may advertise that it offers the lowest interest rate, but then charge more for closing costs and origination fees, thus lessening the appeal as a good value. Some banks will offer you free services such as free checking with direct deposit and/or a free ATM or debit card when you close your mortgage loan with them. This could save you as much as ten to twenty dollars per month in service fees alone. A bank may also be able to offer a discount of their advertised mortgage interest rate by having the new monthly mortgage payment automatically drafted from this new checking account. In addition, you will want to know if your loan will be sold as soon as the mortgage loan is closed. This is important to some people because your mortgage loan could be sold a couple of times within the first two or three years. This may cause you to become confused as to where to mail your mortgage payment. Or the company that the loan is sold to could have a very poor customer service track record.

The next big step in the process is to fill out a mortgage loan application. Completing a loan application is quick and easy if you are prepared to answer the questions. With most companies, you will either complete the loan application in person, over the phone, or even over the Internet. If you complete an application over the phone or via the internet, it is important that the company to which you are applying is a reputable mortgage lender because you are volunteering very valuable information about yourself, such as your social security number and date of birth. If you are applying with a local company over the phone, you can check the local chapter of the Better Business Bureau or ask for references. If you are applying over the Internet, you can check for news articles about the company or view their public information at a number of independent financial web sites. If you are not comfortable applying by these methods, then have the company mail you an application.

The mortgage loan application first provides space where you will list the last two years worth of your residence information and for whom you have worked. When giving the dates of residency or employment, you do not need to know the exact day but only the month and year. For your housing information, you will need to provide the street address(es) where you have lived over the last two years. For your work information, you will need to provide information for whom you have worked over the last two years. You will need to list the phone number or mailing address to the place of business in case the work information needs to be verified. The application has space to show details about your income. (You gathered this information in Chapter Three.) You will then need to provide a list of all your assets: (1) How much money is presently in your checking and/or savings account, (2) how much money is in any retirement or investment accounts, (3) how many and what type of automobile(s) do you own and their approximate values, and (4) any other miscellaneous property or asset you may own with its approximate value will need to be listed. The application has space for you to provide details about what debts you owe and how much you pay each month for those debts. If you are well prepared, then filling out the mortgage application will only take about ten to fifteen minutes and the loan officer will be able to get started immediately in prequalifying you for a mortgage loan. Not being able to completely answer all questions will cause an unnecessary delay in the mortgage loan process.

With each application you complete to prequalify for a mortgage loan, each lender is required to give you, within three business days, an early disclosure package of information if they have not declined your loan. This early disclosure package will have a lot of information in it. You need to read through the material carefully and ask questions about anything you do not understand. **The most important early disclosure form is the Good Faith Estimate.** The Good Faith Estimate will disclose and list what the estimated closing costs will be. Another important early disclosure is the Preliminary Truth in Lending Disclosure. However, you may not receive this disclosure if it is not a required form for the type of loan you are applying. If you do not receive this form, then I would recommend that you request it, if possible, from your lender. The Preliminary Truth in Lending Disclosure will list the interest rate and the monthly payment for the loan. If the lender will not provide you with this disclosure form, then ask him or her to quote you the interest rate and payment information. This information is what you can use to compare the different home equity loan proposals you will be receiving. Shopping around and filling out two or three mortgage loan applications could potentially cause a slight drop in your credit score, if these different lenders each pull your credit report. However, the point drop caused by having a couple of inquiries within a day or two will be very minimal, if any at all.

Key points for you to review in the pre-disclosure packages are:

- What is the interest rate?

- What is the monthly payment?

- What is the loan origination fee?

- What are the total closing costs?

- What is the total cost of the loan (including the principle loan amount, finance charge, and closing costs)?

- Is there a prepayment penalty?

- Does the new loan payment, including the escrow amount, fit easily into my family budget?

Write the answers down on paper and compare them closely. This will help you to choose the mortgage loan officer and the company with whom you will do your mortgage loan. After you have chosen the mortgage lender and loan officer, it is important that you contact any other lenders you may have applied with and withdraw your loan application from consideration. **You can only have one mortgage application pending at one time.**

Once you sign and return the early disclosure package to the lender you have chosen, along with your proof of income, copy of your original deed of trust, copy of your monthly mortgage statement or payment booklet, and proof of homeowner's insurance, the rest of the process shouldn't take more than fifteen to thirty days. After the package is received, the lender will begin verifying your job(s), the previous mortgage history, your credit references and obtaining loan payoffs if you are consolidating any debts. Remember to keep a copy of the early disclosure package so that you can refer to it later.

As a sign of good faith, along with the signed and returned early disclosure package, the lender may require a personal check to cover the cost of the appraisal. That way, should you decide to cancel the mortgage application after the appraisal has been completed, the appraisal will be paid for. That is okay, but if you do decide to cancel the mortgage loan application after the appraisal has been performed, and the lender cashes your check, then you have a right to that appraisal. It is now yours because you have paid for it.

Summary of documents required by lender:

• Signed and returned mortgage application

• Signed and returned early disclosure package

• Copy of the original Deed of Trust to the property

• Proof of income

• Copy of the current first mortgage monthly statement or payment booklet

• Proof of homeowner's insurance

• Copy of monthly statements for any consumer debts being paid off, if the loan is for consolidation purposes

• Personal check to pay for the appraisal, if required by the lender

Remember, if thirty days passes from the time the lender initially pulled your credit report for prequalification until you actually close your loan, the lender might request another credit report prior to closing. At this stage, the loan could still be denied if anything has changed. **So, it is important that you do not inquire anywhere for credit until *after* you sign the new loan note.**

Chapter 7: Understanding the Loan Approval Process

Below is a list of four tasks the lender will probably require. Your mortgage loan officer can explain in greater detail what each task means if you need further explanation. The lender will take care of the first three.

The first task is that an appraisal will probably be performed on the property being used as collateral for the loan. The appraisal will determine what the market value of your home is as compared to recent sales of similar houses in your immediate neighborhood or geographical area. The goal for the appraiser is to match your home against recent sales of similar homes and compare these houses. The appraiser tries to find at least three comparable, or similar, homes to analyze. He analyzes the similarities and differences between your house and the three comparables and comes up with a dollar figure for what the current market conditions indicate that your house is worth. Make sure that the appraiser is licensed to do business in your state and that you get a copy of the appraisal report with your loan closing.

The next task is that the mortgage company will perform a flood search on the physical location of your current house. A flood search is a federal requirement on all mortgage loan transactions where a structure is involved. The purpose of the report is to check to see if the house you own is located in a flood zone. This is very important because if the home is in a flood plain, then you will need to have flood insurance. The flood insurance premium can be very expensive. It is necessary to have flood insurance because the standard homeowner's insurance policy will not insure your house or belongings against any damage caused by a flood.

The third task is that a title search company or a local attorney, who will be doing the loan closing, is to perform a title search on the property at the local courthouse where the property is located. The purpose of the title search is to check and make sure that you are the legal owners of the property and there are no other liens, judgments or encumbrances that might jeopardize the lien position of the mortgage loan. Some mortgage companies may require title insurance to accompany the title search. Title insurance guarantees the lien position and protects the borrower and mortgage company from any claims not identified in the title search. Title insurance is not mandatory on a mortgage loan refinance unless the mortgage company requires it. I would not recommend that you request title insurance yourself because you should have gotten the insurance when you bought the property. If you did not get title insurance when you originally purchased the property, then it might be a good idea to get it now.

The fourth task is that you will have to provide proof to the lender that there is sufficient homeowner's insurance coverage on your house before you can close on your new mortgage loan. This is a good time to review your homeowner's policy to make sure that you have adequate coverage and that the policy includes "replacement cost". Replacement cost means that if your house is damaged or destroyed, that it will be repaired using today's cost (i.e., what it would take to rebuild the house in today's market) not what it cost to originally build.

If you become fortunate and eventually own your home free and clear of any mortgages and/or liens, then it is important that you *keep* homeowner's insurance and flood insurance, if applicable, on the property. Just because there is not a lender requiring any insurance coverage, does not mean that it is a wise choice to let the protection expire. It is important that you continue to properly protect what is probably your largest valued asset, your house, that you worked so hard to own.

Chapter 8: Ready to Close the Loan

The loan is ready to be closed when the information from your loan application has been verified and all necessary reports have been completed. **You should go over the final figures with your mortgage loan officer a day or two prior to going to the closing table.** This review prevents there from being any surprises or last minute changes. If there are any changes, then you will want to take care of them before you get to the closing table. If there are any surprises, or if you uncover anything that you do not agree with, **DO NOT SIGN** the paperwork.

When reviewing the paper work, pay close attention to the Final Settlement Statement. **Make sure all charges and fees listed are very close to what you agreed to.** You can do this by comparing the charges listed on the Final Settlement Statement with the estimated closing cost listed in the Good Faith Estimate Disclosure; you received when you applied for the loan. It is also important to review the Final Truth in Lending (the promissory note) Statement. You should check this form to make sure the total monthly payment, which should include the monthly escrow charges, is what you were expecting. This form should also indicate when the first payment is due. Lastly, check the Deed of Trust to make sure that your name is properly spelled and that the property has been correctly identified.

As a safe guard, when you are refinancing your primary residence, the loan will have a three-day rescission period. This means that you have three business days to cancel the transaction at no cost to you, except for maybe the appraisal fee that was discussed earlier. The three-day rescission period is called a "cooling off" period. This allows you time to review the loan documents thoroughly at your home without any sale pressures. After the three days have expired, the funds (money) will be disbursed and you will then be able to pick up any loan proceed checks. **If you are refinancing a secondary home or an investment property, then there will be no rescission period** so you will want to make sure that everything in the loan is as promised prior to signing.

Congratulations!!

Section III
The Home Equity Loan
(Second Mortgages)

Introduction

The Home Equity Loan section is specifically for the homeowner who is thinking of getting a second mortgage. A second mortgage, or home equity loan, is secured as a lien against the homeowner's primary or secondary residence. This section will help you in three main ways: (1) To understand the differences between the two main types of second mortgages, (2) to understand the second mortgage process, and (3) to help get you the proper home equity loan.

When a borrower goes through the process of getting a first mortgage loan, a mortgage loan officer, possibly with a realtor, guides the borrower along the way. Those resources are not available for you during the second mortgage process. But don't worry, this section will guide you along the way and walk you through the process. In most cases, borrowers will be communicating and working directly with a local bank branch manager or a local finance company representative when applying for and closing a second mortgage loan. However, in other cases, it is possible to apply for a loan over an internet web site or through the mail. If that is the case, then you should have a toll free phone number and contact person whom you can call to discuss the terms of the loan and to answer any questions that you might have. For this type of loan, it is advisable not to obtain the help of a third party mortgage broker because it will add an unnecessary cost to your loan. As a reminder, **a second mortgage loan, or home equity loan, is a lien against your property, just like your first mortgage. If you fail to repay the debt as agreed, you could risk losing your home.**

Chapter 1: Why Should I Get A Second Mortgage?

Years ago, second mortgages were rare. They are, however, very commonplace in today's society. There are six main reasons for this dramatic shift over the last twenty years:

Reason One: Tax Deductible Interest

The first main reason for this change is that interest paid on a consumer loan, such as an automobile loan or a credit card, is no longer tax deductible. On the other hand, interest paid on the home equity loan is potentially tax deductible (please consult your tax advisor). In most cases it will be, but there are some limitations. You can only deduct interest paid on your second mortgage loan up to one hundred percent of the value of your home and up to a loan balance of $100,000.

Reason Two: Easy to Get

A second reason for the surge in popularity of second mortgages is that banks and lending institutions have made it very easy for the typical consumer to get a home equity loan. It is almost as easy to get a second mortgage loan as it is to get an automobile loan (but requires a little more paperwork and a little more money). Borrowers can complete an application in person at the bank, over the phone, through the mail, or even over the internet.

Reason Three: Attractive Interest Rates

The third reason fueling the popularity of second mortgages is that you can generally get better terms for second mortgages when compared to consumer loans (consumer loans are discussed in Section Four). A second mortgage loan will generally have a lower interest rate than a consumer loan because of the collateral being pledged. You can also get an extended repayment term and lower, more affordable, monthly payments with a second mortgage loan. Typically, consumer loans have repayment periods of five years or less, but a home equity loan can have a repayment period as long as fifteen years. Some lending institutions will sometimes make an exception and allow a second mortgage to be amortized over twenty or even thirty years.

Reason Four: Avoid Paying Mortgage Insurance

A fourth reason for people to choose a second mortgage is to avoid having to pay mortgage insurance on their first mortgage loan. Mortgage insurance (also known as private mortgage insurance or PMI) is a monthly insurance premium that is charged to borrowers who have borrowed more than eighty percent of the appraised value of their home and who have a "conventional" first mortgage loan. The mortgage insurance payment is in addition to the monthly principle and interest payment, the homeowner's insurance monthly premium, and the real estate tax bill. (A "conventional" first mortgage loan is a loan where the bank or mortgage broker, after closing your loan, sells the loan, and possibly it's servicing rights, to another bank or financial institution on the secondary market. If the servicing rights to your mortgage loan are sold, then you would make your regular monthly payment to another company.) Mortgage insurance protects the mortgage company from any loss it might incur should you default on your first mortgage loan because it agreed to lend more than the eighty percent of the value of the home. The mortgage insurance premium can be expensive, is not tax deductible, and the benefit is paid to the mortgage company.

As an example, suppose you were *buying* a house for $150,000 and you wanted to avoid paying mortgage insurance, but you have only five percent of the purchase price ($7,500.00) as cash to put toward the down payment. **To avoid paying mortgage insurance you could opt for a first mortgage/second mortgage combination loan,** also called an "80/10/10", "80/15/5", or "80/20" loan. The combination loan means that the first mortgage loan would be for the loan amount equal to eighty percent ("80") of the purchase price of the home. The second number represents what the second mortgage loan balance would be as a percentage of the purchase price of the home, either ten percent ("10"), fifteen percent ("15"), or twenty percent ("20"). The third number represents the amount of cash, as a percentage of the purchase price, that you would be putting down as the down payment, either ten percent ("10"), five percent ("5"), or zero percent. In this example in order to avoid paying mortgage insurance, you would get a first mortgage loan for $120,000 and a "piggy back" second mortgage loan for $22,500 to cover the difference. This type of scenario would also be called an "80/15/5" loan.

$150,000 Purchase Price	$150,000 Purchase Price
x 80% Loan-to-value Limit	-120,000 First Mortgage Amt.
$120,000 First Mortgage Amt.	-7,500 5% Down Payment
	$22,500 Second Mortgage Amt.

People also use this same philosophy, a first mortgage/second mortgage combination loan, when they are *refinancing* a first mortgage loan and they need to borrow more than eighty percent of the value of the home in order to meet their borrowing needs. There are two benefits to this type of first and second mortgage loan structure. The first benefit of this two-loan structure, as previously discussed, is to avoid adding an unnecessary cost, the mortgage insurance premium, to the first mortgage monthly payment. The second benefit is that you can save money by reducing the total finance (interest) cost. That is because interest rates are generally a little lower when borrowing up to eighty percent of the value of your home as compared to getting a ninety or ninety-five percent "loan-to-value" mortgage loan. Loan-to-value is simply the ratio of the principle balance of the mortgage loan divided by the appraised value of your home. The reason for the lower interest rate at eighty percent loan-to-value is that the mortgage company, or bank, is less likely to suffer a loss should you default on the mortgage loan, thus they can pass the savings on to you.

In this example, you are in the process of refinancing your first mortgage loan which has a current loan balance of $135,000. Your house is worth $150,000. You need to borrow 90% of the value of the home in order to refinance.

$135,000 Loan Amount
÷150,000 Market Value of Home
    90%   Loan-to-value

Now, let's compare the two types of loan structures, a first mortgage/second mortgage combination loan and a first mortgage loan. With the **first mortgage/second mortgage combination loan,** the first mortgage loan balance would be $120,000, which is 80% of the value of the home. The second mortgage loan balance, at 10% loan-to-value, would be $15,000.

$150,000 Market Value of Home $150,000 Market Value of Home
 x 80% Loan-to-Value   x 10% Loan-to-Value
$120,000 First Mortgage Loan $15,000 Second Mortgage Loan

The current market interest rate for a thirty year first mortgage loan at the eighty-percent loan-to-value threshold is 8%. Looking at an amortization table, the total finance charge (interest) for the first mortgage loan is $197,000. The interest rate being offered on the second mortgage loan for a 10-year term is 9.5%. The total finance charge from the amortization table is $8,292. So the total cost of the first mortgage/second mortgage combination loan is $205,292 and the interest paid on both mortgage loans is tax deductible. This type of scenario would also be called an "80/10" loan.

$197,000 Finance Charge, First Mortgage
 +8,292 Finance Charge, Second Mortgage
$205,292 Total Finance Charge, *Combination Loan*

Now, let's suppose that you decide to get only a **first mortgage loan** for the total amount needed. You find that for a thirty-year mortgage loan at 90% loan-to-value, the interest rate you are being offered is 8.25%. Looking at an amortization table, the total finance charge for the loan will be $230,115. You will *also* have to pay mortgage insurance on the loan because you are borrowing more than 80% of the value of home and you are getting a conventional mortgage loan. This will cost an extra $87.75 per month for a total of approximately $4,212 over the first four years of your mortgage loan, which is the approximate length of time (for this example) needed to get the mortgage loan balance below the eighty-percent loan-to-value threshold so the mortgage insurance can be dropped. (For this example, the mortgage insurance premium, PMI, is estimated at $.65 per $1000 of your loan balance.)

$135,000 Loan Balance	$135.00
÷1,000 Of Value	x $.65 PMI Value
$135.00	X 48 Months (4 years)
	$4,212.00 PMI Cost over 4 years

Therefore getting the first mortgage/second mortgage combination loan ("80/10" loan) will save you $29,035 in finance charges (interest) over the life of the loan as compared to the first mortgage loan. However, sometimes the combination loan will have a higher combined monthly payment than the first mortgage loan. So you need to make sure that the monthly payments fit your family budget.

$230,115 Finance Charge, First Mortgage
+4,212 PMI Cost Over 4 years, First Mortgage
-205,292 Total Finance Charge, Combination Loan
$29,035 Total Savings, *Combination Loan*

Reason Five: Avoid Jumbo Loans

A fifth reason for people to take advantage of a second mortgage loan is to avoid paying the higher interest rate that is associated with "jumbo" loans. A jumbo mortgage loan is another term for a very large conventional first mortgage loan. The current threshold for a mortgage loan to be qualified as a "jumbo" loan is a principle loan balance of more than $322,700, as of January, 2003. These large loans have a slightly higher interest rate than a conventional mortgage loan and therefore will be more expensive in terms of total finance charges. The jumbo mortgage loan rate is sometimes a quarter or a half percentage point higher than the conventional first mortgage loan rate, with a balance of $322,700 or less.

As an example, suppose you were buying a house for $450,000. You had the 20% cash down payment requirement to avoid paying the mortgage insurance premium, but you also wanted to avoid paying the higher jumbo loan interest rate. Therefore, in order to get the lower interest rate, the maximum amount for which the first mortgage loan could be is $322,700. The down payment amount would be $90,000, which makes the second mortgage loan balance $37,300. If you were to get only a first mortgage jumbo loan at the eighty percent loan-to-value threshold, then the first mortgage loan balance would be $360,000.

$450,000 Purchase Price	$450,000 Purchase Price
X 20%	-322,700 First Mortgage Amt.
$90,000 Down Payment Amt.	-90,000 Down Payment Amt.
	$37,300 Second Mortgage Amt.

Reason Six: To Consolidate Debt

The sixth and most popular reason for people to get a second mortgage on their home is to save money by consolidating their consumer debt. If you have accumulated equity in your house, or your house has substantially appreciated in value, then you can use that equity in your house to consolidate your consumer debts. You can save money via reducing your ***monthly payments*** (by ***lengthening*** the repayment term) or you can save money via reducing ***the total finance charge*** or interest expense (by ***shortening*** the repayment term).

To illustrate how money can be saved by consolidating consumer debt, let's create a scenario involving Marshall and Maria Johnson. They have been living in their home for five years. Over that time, their property has increased in value to $150,000. The Johnsons have been paying on the original first mortgage loan for these five years and the remaining principle balance owed is now $110,000 at an interest rate of 8%. Maria hears that the market interest rate for a first mortgage loan is now 7.5% and the interest rate for a second mortgage loan is 9%. The Johnsons are only planning to remain in their house for another *five to seven* years. Over the last two years they have accumulated $38,000 in consumer debt.

Marshall reviewed Section Two, Chapter One, of this book and he determined that it is not financially beneficial to refinance their first mortgage loan because of the short time they plan to remain in their home and the fact that mortgage interest rates have only dropped one half of a percentage point. Instead of refinancing, Marshall and Maria decide to get a second mortgage loan. By doing some calculating, they have determined that they have $40,000 of equity in their house, enough to cover their consumer loan debt.

$150,000 Market Value of Home
-110,000 First Mortgage Balance
$40,000 Johnson's Equity

The Johnsons have two possibilities for saving money. The first possibility is to save money by **reducing their total monthly payments**. The second possibility is to save money by **reducing their total finance charge**, or interest expense. The best part is that with either loan option the Johnsons choose, they will save money and increase their tax deductions (because interest paid on a home equity loan is potentially tax deductible). The grand total of overall savings will be even higher after the extra tax savings from their federal income tax return is added in!

Before we look at which possibility for saving money the Johnsons will choose, we need to take a closer look at the $38,000 in consumer loans that they owe. Over the past two years, the Johnsons have charged up $18,000 in credit card debt on three separate cards. Additionally, they recently completed cosmetic remodeling to their kitchen. They bought a couple of new appliances and they took a long vacation over the summer. The average interest rate of the three credit cards is 9.9%. Looking at an amortization table, it would take approximately 212 months, more than fifteen years to pay off these balances if the Johnsons were to only pay the minimum monthly payment of $180.00 per month. (Note: The $180.00 per month used in this example is an overall average for the whole repayment term. You would pay approximately $250.00 to $300.00 at the beginning of your repayment term, when the loan balances were at their highest level, and approximately $50.00 towards the end of the repayment term when the balances are almost paid off.) This would cost the Johnsons about $20,170 in finance charges! The total repayment amount including principle and interest would be $38,170.

Before Marshall and Maria have a chance to get the second mortgage, a few unexpected events take place that affect their financial situation. One of their older cars has broken down, so they had to purchase a new car and have found a good one for $15,000 at a 6% interest rate. They decided to finance the car for 48 months, making their monthly payment $352.00. The total cost of the car loan is $16,909, which includes $1,909 in finance charges.

Also, Marshall's elderly mother is in immediate need of financial assistance, so the Johnsons got an unsecured personal loan for $5,000 at 14.95%. They have financed this loan for 36 months for a monthly payment of $173.00. The total cost of this loan is $6,235, which includes $1,235 in finance charges.

$18,000 Credit Card Debt	$180.00 Credit Card Pmt.
+15,000 Car Loan	+352.00 Car Loan Pmt.
+5,000 Personal Loan	+173.00 Personal Loan Pmt.
$38,000 Total Debts	$705.00 Total Monthly Payments

As shown above, the Johnsons owe $38,000 in total consumer debt. The consumer loans listed above are costing them a total of $705.00 per month. The total repayment of all five loans will be approximately $61,314, which includes $23,314 in non-tax deductible interest (finance charge).

$20,170 Credit Card	$38,170 Credit Card
+1,909 Car Loan	+16,909 Car Loan
+1,235 Personal Loan	+6,235 Personal Loan
$23,314 Total Fin. Charge	$61,314 Total Repayment of Loans

Once these unexpected financial events have passed, Marshall and Maria decide to take action and make the equity in their house start working for them. The Johnsons have already determined that they have enough equity in their house to consolidate all five consumer loans. They know how much they are paying each month for all five loans, and they know the total amount that these loans will cost to individually repay. The Johnsons begin to investigate the two possibilities available to them for saving money through a second mortgage. They are both explained below.

Save Money by *Extending* the Loan Term

This first possibility is to save money by reducing their total monthly payments. This is done by *extending* the repayment term to ten years. To investigate this option, Maria goes online to **www.theborrowingmoneyguide.com** to find a link to an amortization table. The table she locates indicates that a $38,000 home equity loan at 9% for 10 years will cost them $481 per month. The total repayment of the loan is $57,760. The total finance charge, or cost of the loan, is $19,760. Thus, if the Johnsons were to get a ten-year home equity loan, it would save them $224.00 per month and save them $3,554 in total finance charges.

$705.00 Loan Payments	$61,314 Repayment of Loans
-481.00 Equity Loan Pmt.	-57,760 Repayment, Equity Loan
$224.00 Savings Per Month	$3,554 Total Savings

Save Money by *Reducing* the Loan Term

The Johnsons second possibility is to save money by reducing the total finance charge, or interest expense, that they will have paid over the entire length of the individual loans. They would do this by *shortening* the repayment term enough so that the consolidation loan's monthly payment comes close *to matching* the total monthly payment of the five consumer loans. The Johnsons look at the amortization table once again. They find that if they refinance the same $38,000 at 9% for only 6 years, then the monthly payment would be $685.00. By doing further comparisons, they found that the total repayment for the loan would be $49,300 and the total finance charge would only be $11,300! So, by reducing the term of the home equity loan to 6 years, the Johnsons can triple the savings in finance charges (interest cost). The six-year loan term will save them only $20.00 per month, but it will save them a total of $12,014 in finance charges!

$705.00 Loan Payments	$61,314 Repayment of Loans
-685.00 Equity Loan Pmt.	-49,300 Repayment, Equity Loan
$20.00 Savings Per Month	$12,014 Total Savings

In the two examples listed, I would recommend that the Johnsons choose the second example if they can afford to pay the $685.00 monthly payment. This is because they plan on moving within the next five to seven years and the consolidation loan would be almost paid off by the time they considered moving. In addition, they could potentially be debt free going into their next home. Another benefit is that they would have plenty of equity in their house again that could be used as the down payment on the next home purchase.

To summarize, **the key to saving money is to determine what is best for your present financial situation and how the monthly payments affect your monthly family budget.** I recommend that if your family budget can tolerate paying more per month, then you should look at getting a shortened loan term. However, if you know that you will be having some extra monthly expenses added to your family budget such as the birth of a new baby, medical bills for an upcoming surgery, or college expenses, then you should lengthen the loan term to lower your monthly payment. A third possibility is to get an in-between loan term that does a little of both; saves money each month and saves money in total finance cost. That would be an eight-year loan term for the example listed above.

Chapter 2: Getting Your Financial Affairs in Order

In order to get the second mortgage loan you want, as with any other type of loan, you need to make sure your credit is in the best shape possible. **The better your credit is, the better the interest rate for which you will be approved and the more equity in your home you will be able to use.** Most lenders offer loan programs that allow you to borrow up to one hundred percent (as with the example shown in Chapter One) of the value of your home. There are also a few lenders that will allow you to borrow more than one hundred percent of the value of your home. If you do borrow that much, then the interest rate charged will be much higher than a traditional second mortgage interest rate and the interest paid on the portion of the loan that is above the value of your home is generally not tax deductible.

If you think you have established good credit and have paid your bills on time, then you may be tempted to skip ahead to the next chapter. But don't fool yourself, you might have credit blemishes or "slow pay" history in your credit file that you may not be aware of. Also, it is possible that some company could have erroneously reported delinquencies to your credit file. For these reasons, it is advisable that you continue reading. These credit blemishes or "slow pay" histories will be uncovered by the loan officer and with no explanation it could cause your loan to be declined or approved at a higher interest rate. Most lenders will be sympathetic if you tell them during the loan application that there are some credit blemishes. This way you can provide a specific and valid reason for the delinquency other than irresponsibility (if that is not the case). If you have recent late payments or current delinquencies, you may still be able to get a second mortgage loan but the delinquent debts will have to be paid off.

If you have not reviewed your credit report in over a year it is advisable to review it now. You can request a copy of your credit file by contacting one of the three major credit bureau reporting agencies (Equifax, Experian or TransUnion) listed at the end of Section Six, Chapter Four. The credit report should cost you less than fifteen dollars, but it is well worth it. A few states have a law that allows you to request and review a copy of your credit file free of charge at least once a year.

When you receive your credit file, check the report closely for any discrepancies or errors. If there are any errors or disputed delinquencies, you will be able to dispute those references and accounts through the credit bureau agency where you ordered the report. Along with the credit report package will be a form and information on how to go about disputing any data contained in the report. Another way to dispute the credit reference is to contact the creditor directly. **If you have contacted the creditor directly and a representative has agreed to correct the error, make**

sure that you get the correction *in writing*. I have seen many situations in which a borrower will state on a loan application that a collection has been paid off or that a late payment error has been corrected, but comes to find out that the creditor has not reported the correct information to any credit bureau. Other times, the information might only get reported to one of the credit bureau agencies, but not the one being used for this loan. This could either cause a delay in the verification process, cause the loan to be declined, or cause the credit reference to remain against you thereby requiring you to pay a higher interest rate. **As a rule, you should keep any correspondence, including written corrected account information, for at least the next five to seven years.**

If you have filed a bankruptcy in the last ten years, you should get your bankruptcy discharge paperwork together. You might not need them if your bankruptcy was discharged over five years ago, but it is best to be prepared so that if they are required, the loan process will not be delayed. Another reason you may need your bankruptcy discharge paperwork is that perhaps not all of the credit that was included in the bankruptcy was reported properly. Some creditors might continue to show an account as delinquent, indicating that you still owe them money, or as if they charged off your account when, in fact, it was discharged in the bankruptcy and you are no longer responsible for that particular debt. By having your bankruptcy discharge paperwork readily available, you will be able to prove what debts were actually part of the bankruptcy filing. In addition, be prepared to discuss why you filed a bankruptcy in the first place or why you have had any late payments.

To summarize how to get your financial affairs in order:

- Order a copy of your credit file from one of the three main credit reporting agencies.

- Ensure that all of the information being reported is accurate. Make corrections if needed and get it in writing.
- If you have any current delinquencies, you need to pay them current or pay them off with the equity loan.
- If you filed a bankruptcy within the last ten years, then have your bankruptcy discharge papers available.

Chapter 3: Documenting Your Income

Some banks and financial institutions now offer a streamlined second mortgage process that does not require proof of income for people who have very good or above average credit. However, this process is typically reserved for people who have a good relationship with that particular bank or lending institution. Every company is different when it comes to what type of income documentation it requires, so it is best to be prepared.

You will need to be able to prove how much income you make on a *regular* and *consistent* basis. If you are an hourly or salary employee, you will need to have your last two paychecks and the last two years of your W-2 Wage and Tax Statements on hand. If you are an hourly employee and receive any overtime, you will need to be able to prove the income has been consistent over the last two or more years. Most lenders will not include additional income if it is only seasonal or inconsistent. If you are a salary employee who consistently receives a regular quarterly or yearly bonus, you will need to prove that you receive that extra income on a consistent basis as well. This can be done by using the year-to-date gross income from your most recent paycheck and then averaging it with either the last year or two of your W-2 Wage and Tax Statements. **However, it is not a good idea to use any overtime or bonus income to qualify for a loan.** When the overtime is stopped or the bonus income is gone, you might not be able to afford your present debt load or your current standard of living. This could have a damaging effect on your credit rating and your credit score that you worked so hard to build. It is also not a good idea to base your family budget on this extra income.

If you are a "commission only" salesperson, you will need to be able to prove your income in the same manner as the salary employee does. **With commission income, an underwriter is looking for what your *average income* has been over the last two or more years, not what your best month or quarter has been.** If you have just started a new job and will be paid primarily by commissions or large bonuses, then it would be best to conservatively estimate the income that you will be claiming on the home equity loan application. If you have just changed professions and started a new job as a commission only employee (i.e., going from a school teacher to a commission real estate agent), then you may have to postpone the loan request until your income has stabilized and you have been on the job for at least twelve months. In any event, **it is always best to apply for a home equity loan and let the lender review your income situation.**

Being self-employed is sometimes a more complicated situation when it comes to verifying your income. One reason is because self-employed people generally fall into two categories based on the way they report their income on their federal tax returns. They can either report the true income (sales) from their business, with the proper deductions and expenses, and pay the proper federal and state income taxes or they can not report the true income, inflate the deductibles and expenses as much as possible, thereby greatly reducing their tax obligations. **As a self-employed borrower, you will qualify for a mortgage loan a lot easier if an underwriter can use your adjusted gross income listed at the bottom of the first page of your 1040 Federal Income Tax Returns.** In some cases, the underwriter or lender will be able to add back to your adjusted gross income any depreciation or interest expense you may have claimed. Each lender has an internal analysis on how they review self-employment income and business debt. To reiterate, as a self-employed borrower, you will qualify for the best rates if an underwriter or lender can use the income directly from your federal tax returns with little or no manipulations or adjustments. Therefore, you should have on hand the last two years of your federal tax returns with all schedules along with the last couple of months of business bank statements, in case they are required.

If you "hide" your income in order to avoid paying federal income taxes, then you might have to use an alternative method to prove your income and you might have to search for a non-traditional second mortgage lender. There are lenders who offer special loan programs that do not require any proof of income, commonly known as "no-doc" loans, or have flexible income requirements. These types of loans come with higher interest rates, generally have higher fees, and reduce loan sizes. Typically, when attempting to qualify for these alternative types of loans, you will need some combination of federal tax returns, bank statements, a financial statement, and a Profit and Loss Statement for your company.

The purpose of the Profit and Loss Statement is to show the lender how your business is performing over the last quarter or last twelve months. To support the gross income, or sales, that you have claimed for the current year on the Profit and Loss Statement, you will need to have your last six to twelve months of business bank statements on hand. The reason the bank statements are important is that they act as your pay stub. Typically, when you receive money from a customer for goods purchased or services rendered, you deposit the money into a particular business checking account similar to a wage earner depositing his regular weekly paycheck. Then the bills are paid from that business checking account. For this reason, it is recommended that you keep separate checking or deposit accounts for your business and your personal use.

An example of a simple Profit and Loss Statement looks like this:

ABC Company
1/1/04 through 8/30/04

Gross Receipts or Sales		$200,000
Cost of Goods Sold (materials)		($85,000)
Gross Profit		$115,000
Expenses		
Wages & Salaries	$40,000	
Automotive Expenses	$15,000	
Other Expenses	$10,000	
Total Expenses		($65,000)
Net Income		$50,000

By law, you do not have to disclose whether you receive any child support or alimony payments unless you need that additional income to qualify for the loan. If you do receive child support or alimony from an ex-spouse and you plan on claiming that income in your application, you will need to be able to prove that you receive the support payments on a *regular* and *consistent* basis. You can make a copy of the last couple of support checks you have received or you can get your last six to twelve months of bank statements together that shows the support income is being consistently received. It is also a good idea to get a copy of the court ordered support paperwork, or the signed and recorded divorce decree, to add additional support to the income you are claiming. However, you might not be able to use child support income if the dependent will be reaching adult status, typically eighteen years of age, in the near future. Also, alimony income might not be able to be used if the income has certain restrictions such as getting remarried or a termination date that is in the near future.

If you are on a fixed income or you receive a subsidized income (i.e., social security, disability, workman's compensation, or retirement income to name a few), then you will need to be able to prove how much money you receive on a *monthly* and *consistent* basis and *how long* you will be receiving it. You will need to get your last year's 1099 Federal Wage Form and the most recent award letter or monthly check stub together. If you have direct deposit for this money, then you can use the last two months of your bank statements. Depending on the type of income you receive, you might also have to get a letter from your employer, or from the source of that income, stating how long this income is expected to continue.

By law, you cannot be discriminated against for the type of income you receive. **The key is being able to verify that whatever income you are receiving and using to qualify for the home equity loan, will be consistently received by you on a regular and ongoing basis.** You should never let your income discourage you from applying for a loan. It is always best to apply for the loan, provide proof of your income, and let the lender determine how much income is verifiable and can be used with your loan application.

To summarize documenting your income:

- For an hourly or salary employee, you will need a copy of your last two paychecks and last two years of your W-2 Wage and Tax Statement.
- For a commission sales person, you will need a copy of your last two paychecks and last two years of your W-2 Wage and Tax Statement.
- For a self-employed person, who does not "hide" his or her income, you should have the last two years of your federal tax returns with all schedules along with the last couple months of business bank statements, in case they are required.

- For a self-employed person qualifying for a non-traditional or alternative loan program, you should have the last two years of your federal tax returns with all schedules along with a Profit and Loss Statement for your company, a financial statement, and the last six to twelve months of business bank statements.

- For an individual using support income, you will need a copy of the section from the divorce decree which outlines the support payments, a copy of the last two support checks, and the last six months of your bank statements.

- For an individual who receives a fixed or subsidized income, you will need a copy of the most recent award letter, the last year of the 1099 Federal Wage and Tax Form, the last two months of your bank statements, and the last two years of your federal tax returns.

Chapter 4: How Do I Choose the Right Loan?

Fantastic! Up to this point, you have been busy deciding why you need to get a second mortgage loan, reviewing your credit, and gathering your income documentation together. The next step is to decide what type of second mortgage or home equity loan you want that will best meet your current and/or future borrowing needs. There are only two types of second mortgage loans for the typical consumer to choose from. There is the basic Second Mortgage (Equity) Loan and The Home Equity Line of Credit (commonly known as a HELOC). Banks and lending institutions have given these loans some very creative names and use various marketing gimmicks to sell them, but they are all similar in nature.

The Basic Second Mortgage (Equity) Loan

The Second Mortgage Loan, also known as a Home Equity Loa n, is the easier of the two to understand. It is very similar to the Fixed Rate First Mortgage Loan you read about in Section Two, if you refinanced your first mortgage loan. With the Second Mortgage Equity Loan, all of the money is borrowed up front in one lump sum. The loan will be repaid with a fixed monthly payment, with a fixed interest rate and for a fixed term. The repayment term for this type of loan is generally five to fifteen years. The examples listed in this section are of this type of loan.

This type of loan is primarily for those who have a one-time event for which they need money. This loan would be ideal for someone who needs money in order to consolidate their consumer debt, has a small home improvement project, or needs the cash for an isolated event such as an auto purchase, major surgery, or a wedding. This type of loan is also best suited for someone on a limited or fixed income so the monthly payment can be easily planned into his or her family budget. The drawbacks are that if you need to borrow more money in the future, you will have to apply for another loan and the current Home Equity Loan will have to be refinanced.

Typically, it is undesirable to get a balloon amortization term with the Home Equity Loan. It is best to have the Home Equity Loan fully amortized with no prepayment penalty. The reason is when the balloon loan matures, there will be a balance remaining that either must be paid off with cash, refinanced into another new equity loan, or the property would have to be sold to satisfy the remaining debt. A balloon loan is best suited as a first mortgage loan, which is further explained in Section Two, Chapter Four.

The Home Equity Line of Credit (HELOC)

The second type of second mortgage loan is the Home Equity Line of Credit, also known as the HELOC. This type of loan can be equated to a tax-deductible credit card. The HELOC is similar to a credit card because it is a revolving line of credit used primarily for purchases and cash advances. What differentiates this loan from a credit card is that this line of credit is secured as a lien against your home and there are typically no fees involved for cash advances. With the line of credit you will typically be given a checkbook, so that when you want to purchase something or to get a cash advance, you would write a check instead of using a plastic card. (There are now a few companies who offer ATM or credit cards with their HELOC loans but you need to be aware of any cash advance or usage fees they may have.)

The HELOC loan typically will have a variable interest rate that is tied to either the U.S. Prime Rate or the LIBOR (London Interbank Offered Rate). These base rates are interest rates that large financial institutions charge other banks (or their best, most creditworthy, large commercial or industrial customers) for short-term commercial notes. Most banks or financial institutions will charge its borrowers, like you and me, an interest rate that is near the base rate or slightly higher. The difference between the base interest rate and the interest rate charged for the line of credit is called the "margin" or "spread".

As an example, let's assume that the current U.S. Prime Interest Rate is 6%. You have inquired at the local bank where you have your checking account and the bank is offering its customers a variable interest rate of 7% for their Home Equity Lines of Credit. That means that the margin (spread) for the bank's HELOC loan is 1% or "prime plus one". When you are comparing interest rates, you will need to know what this margin rate (spread) is. What makes the HELOC attractive in the short-term is that your variable interest rate will be lower initially than the fixed interest rate associated with the Home Equity Loan. If you recall, the examples listed in Chapter Two of this section had fixed interest rates for Home Equity Loans between 9 and 9.5 percent. However, if interest rates rise in the future, your variable rate loan will increase accordingly and could potentially cost you more than the fixed rate Home Equity Loan that you were originally offered.

An important part of obtaining a line of credit is to make sure that you get a **Home Equity Line of Credit for which you can afford the minimum monthly payment at its *highest point*, or *maximum credit line*.** Therefore, the line of credit should be between ten thousand and fifty thousand dollars for a typical consumer who makes between twenty-five to seventy-five thousand dollars per year in annual income. The Home Equity Line of Credit is for people who have current, along with future, borrowing needs. These needs could consist of paying yearly college expenses, paying for ongoing renovations to a home, or buying a number of large high cost items, such as a used car or new appliances, over the next couple of years. The HELOC could also be used to help steady your cash flow if you are a small business owner or a commission sales person. I recommend this loan for people who can manage their revolving credit (credit cards), want easy access to cash, and are financially responsible.

There are a couple of things that you need to find out about the Home Equity Line of Credit from the lender. Some questions you should ask the lender are:

- What will the base interest rate be tied to (as explained on the previous page)?
- How often will my interest rate change? (Most HELOC loans will change monthly or every six months.)
- What is the margin (spread) associated with this loan? (Meaning how much higher is my rate over the base rate.)

- How high can the variable interest rate go? (Most lines of credit will have a rate cap of anywhere from eighteen to twenty-four percent. But the margin rate will always keep the same spread between the base rate and your interest rate.)
- How do I access cash? (Most HELOC loans have a variety of ways to access the cash. Cash advances can be made by telephone, in person at the branch, by depositing a check through the ATM, or over the internet. Some HELOC loans now come with there own ATM card. Make sure that there are no cash advance fees or annual fees associated with the line.)
- What is the minimum cash advance amount I can request? (Most HELOC loans come with a minimum cash advance of between one hundred and five hundred dollars.)
- How long can I access the cash in my Home Equity Line of Credit? (Some HELOC loans can have time restrictions such as three years, five years, or fifteen years.)
- If my equity line does have a cash advance time restriction, then what happens after my line of credit is closed to cash advances? (You will need to know how your are expected to repay any loan balance after the cash advance period has expired.)
- The most important question to ask is: How is my minimum monthly payment determined?

Now that you know the characteristics of the two types of second mortgages, you have a good understanding of which equity loan is right for you. Listed below are the key questions to ask yourself in order to finally decide which mortgage is the right one for you and your financial situation.

- Why do I need this loan?
- What am I going to do with the money?
- Will I have any need to borrow more money in the near future?

- How long do I plan on staying in this house?

This last question is key, because either type of loan counts as a lien on your property. If you decide to sell your home, then this loan would have to be paid off in full, along with your first mortgage loan. If you were counting on using the equity in your home as a down payment source for your next home, then you might want to reconsider getting a second mortgage, borrow a lesser amount, or borrow for a shorter amount of time to preserve some equity.

The key difference between the two loan types is the interest rate. If the interest rate is fixed, then typically the loan is a closed end Home Equity Loan. This means that the monthly payments will not change throughout the term of the loan. If the interest rate is variable, then most likely the loan is a Home Equity Line of Credit. This means that the loan terms and monthly payment will change throughout the term of the loan.

Chapter 5: Tips and Pointers

Tip 1: A shorter loan term saves money

For the Home Equity Loan, the shorter the mortgage term, the more money you will save in total cost or finance charges. This can be very substantial as with the example discussed in Chapter One. You should look at two or three different loan terms in order to determine which monthly payment fits best in your family budget. If you are requesting a ten-year loan, then ask the lender for the monthly payment and total repayment or payback (the principle amount borrowed plus the finance charge) for a five-year, seven-year, or eight-year loan and compare.

Tip 2: Be careful of over equity or 125% equity loans

There are a few lenders that offer "over" equity loans, or loans that allow you to borrow over one hundred percent of the value of your home. These lenders allow you to borrow up to one hundred and twenty-five percent of the value of your home. But, this type of loan has three major drawbacks. The first drawback is that you will be stuck in your home for the next couple of years until the combined balances of the first and second mortgage loans are below the value of your home. The second drawback is that the rates offered for these "over" equity loans are substantially higher than a traditional second mortgage loan because of the increased risk the lender is willing to accept. The third and final major drawback for this type of loan is that the interest paid on the portion of the loan that is above the value of your home is generally not tax deductible.

Tip 3: Avoid prepayment penalties

Ask about prepayment penalties. A prepayment penalty is a fee paid to the lender for the privilege of paying off the loan prior to maturity to compensate the lender for loss of future income from the loan. The fee is usually one to three percent of the loan amount, which is payable to the lender at the time of payoff. Most prepayment terms are for three or five years. However, some states do not allow prepayment penalties on a second mortgage loan. It is recommended that your loan does NOT have a prepayment penalty. If your loan does have a prepayment penalty, then you can try and negotiate the prepayment term for a shorter period of time or apply with another lender and compare.

Tip 4: Know what your closing costs are

Find out from the lender if the closing costs need to be paid out of your own pocket or are they included in the loan. The closing costs will initially be disclosed on the Good Faith Estimate that you will get from the lender when you apply for the loan. The Good Faith Estimate will show you how many points (origination fee) the lender is charging you and what other closing costs are associated with the loan. Most second mortgage loans come with between one to three points. However, some lenders do offer equity loans with no origination fee or points. A point (or origination fee) is one percent of the loan amount. As an example, if you are being charged two points on your loan and you borrow $20,000.00 then the origination fee will be $400.00 ($20,000 x .02 = $400.00). However, the origination fee is tax deductible.

Tip 5: Do <u>not</u> reuse credit cards after they have been paid off by a consolidation loan

If you are paying off credit card debt or other consumer loans with a new second mortgage loan, then you cannot go back and run up those lines of credit again. **The key to a successful consolidation loan is to save money by *eliminating* the other debt and having only one monthly payment.** If you do decide to reuse those charge cards again and run up debt, you will be in worse financial trouble and most likely you will not have the equity in your house to bail you out again.

Tip 6: Continue to pay the regular monthly payment on all debts until the new loan closes

It is important that if you are paying off debt with this loan that you *continue* to pay the regular monthly payments on all your loans, even the loans that are being paid off, until you actually close your loan. **Even if the loan officer tells you otherwise,** there could always be a delay with the loan closing or the checks could get mailed to a wrong address. If this happens and the creditor does not receive a monthly payment (or the loan payoff) by the due date, then the loan *will* get reported as being delinquent. This would cause your credit score to drop and possibly cause you problems with qualify for future loans.

Tip 7: Get a due date that works well with your family budget

Discuss a payment due date with your lender. If you get paid once a month, then you will want a due date that falls a couple of days *after* you get paid to allow time for mailing. If you get a paycheck every week, twice a month, or every two weeks, then **you will want a due date that falls between the sixteenth to the twenty-first of the month.** The reason you want the due date for the second mortgage loan towards the middle of the month is because most first mortgage loans are due on the first day of the month. Since the second mortgage will probably be your second largest family bill, you do not want the monthly mortgage payments overlapping. If they do, it might cause one of the bills to always be paid late, incur unnecessary late fees, and potentially harm your credit score. A good lender will know to adjust the due date for the second mortgage loan in order to accommodate your monthly family budget.

Chapter 6: Understanding the Loan Approval Process

You are now ready to start the loan approval process. The first step is to gather a short list of potential mortgage lenders. To find a mortgage lender, do some research to get at least two or three rate quotes. One place to check interest rates is at a lender's web site. Another option is to contact the local branch manager where you do your banking business and have your checking account. In addition, you could check with the business section of your local newspaper. You will want to compare the mortgage interest rates, prepaid points (commonly known as origination fees) and closing costs (such as processing fee, attorney fee, application fee, document preparation fee, and appraisal fee, to name a few). Choose the lender you are most comfortable with and/or gives you the best overall deal.

Sometimes the lender who offers you the lowest interest rate may not be offering the best overall *value***.** A lending company may advertise that it offers the lowest interest rate, but then charge more for closing costs and origination fees, thus lessening the appeal as a good value. Some banks will offer you free services such as free checking with direct deposit and/or a free ATM or debit card when you close your equity loan with them. This could save you as much as ten to twenty dollars per month in service fees alone. A bank may also be able to offer a discount of their advertised home equity loan interest rate by having the new monthly payment automatically drafted from this new checking account.

Applying for the Loan

By this stage of the process, you have decided on the loan program you want and have your income documents together. It is now time to complete a loan application. Completing a loan application is quick and easy if you are prepared to answer the questions. With most companies, you will either complete the loan application in person, over the phone, or even over the Internet. If you complete an application over the phone or the internet, it is important that the company you are applying with is a reputable lender because you are volunteering very valuable information about yourself, such as your social security number and date of birth. If you are applying with a local company over the phone, you can check the local chapter of the Better Business Bureau or ask for references. If you are applying over the Internet, you can check for news articles about the company or view the company's public information at a number of financial web sites. If you are not comfortable applying in these manners, then have the company mail you an application.

The loan application first provides space where you will list the last two years worth of your residence information and for whom you have worked. When giving the dates of residency or employment, you do not need to know the exact day, but only the month and year. For your housing information, you will need to provide the street address(es) where you have lived over the last two years. For your work information, you will need to provide information for whom you have worked over the last two years. You will need to list the phone number or mailing address to the place of business in case the work information needs to be verified. The application has space to show details about your income. (You gathered this information in Chapter Three.) You will then need to provide a list of all your assets: (1) How much money is presently in your checking and/or savings account, (2) how much money you have in any retirement or investment accounts, (3) how many and what type of automobile(s) you own and their approximate values, and (4) any other miscellaneous property or asset you may own with its approximate value will need to be listed. The application has space for you to provide details about what debts you owe and how much you pay each month for those debts. If you are well prepared, then filling out the loan application will only take about ten to fifteen minutes and the lender will be able to get started immediately in underwriting your equity loan. Not being able to completely answer all questions will cause an unnecessary delay in the loan process.

With each application you complete, each lender is required to give you, within three business days, an early disclosure package of information if they have not declined your loan. This pre-disclosure package will have a lot of information in it. You need to read through the material carefully and ask questions about anything you do not understand. The most important early disclosure form is the Good Faith Estimate. The Good Faith Estimate will disclose and list what the estimated closing costs will be. Another important early disclosure is the Preliminary Truth in Lending Disclosure. However, you may not receive this disclosure if it is not a required form for the type of loan you are applying. If you do not receive this form, then I would recommend that you request it, if possible, from your lender. The Preliminary Truth in Lending Disclosure will list the interest rate and the monthly payment for the loan. If the lender will not provide you with this disclosure form, then ask him or her to quote you the interest rate and payment information. This information is what you can use to compare the different home equity loan proposals you will be receiving. Shopping around and filling out two or three loan applications could potentially cause a slight drop in your credit score, if these different lenders each pull your credit report. However, the point drop caused by having a couple of inquiries within a day or two will be very minimal, if any at all.

Points for you to review in the pre-disclosure packages are:

- What is the interest rate?
- What is the monthly payment?
- What is the loan origination fee?
- What are the total closing costs?
- What is the total cost of the loan (including the principle loan amount, finance charge, and closing costs)?
- Is there a prepayment penalty?

- Does the new loan payment fit easily into my family budget?

Write the answers down on paper and compare them closely. This will help you choose the lender and the company with whom you will do your equity loan. After you have chosen the lender, it is important that you contact any other lenders you may have applied with and withdraw your loan application from consideration. **You can only have one home equity loan application pending at one time.**

Once you have decided on a lender and loan company, you will be required to sign and return the early disclosure package you initially received along with the required documents as requested by the lender. Some of the required documents may include: proof of income, copy of your original deed of trust, a copy of your first mortgage monthly statement or payment booklet, proof of homeowner's insurance, and copies of the monthly statement for any consumer loans you plan on paying off. Remember to keep a copy of the early disclosure package for yourself so you can refer to it later. At this point, the process should not take more than a couple of days and no longer than three weeks to complete. Remember, **it is important that you** *continue* **to pay the regular monthly payment on all your loans, even the loans that are being paid off, until you actually close on the new loan.**

Summary of documents required by lender:

- Signed and returned loan application
- Signed and returned early disclosure package
- Copy of the original Deed of Trust to the property
- Proof of income
- Copy of the first mortgage monthly statement or payment booklet
- Proof of homeowner's insurance
- Copy of monthly statements for any consumer debts being paid off, if the loan is for consolidation purposes

• Personal check to pay for the Appraisal, if required by lender

As a sign of good faith, the lender may require, along with the signed and returned pre-disclosure package, a personal check to cover the cost of the appraisal if one needs to be performed. That way should you decide to cancel the equity loan after the appraisal has been completed the appraisal will be paid for. That is okay, but if you do decide to cancel the loan application after the appraisal has been performed, and the lender cashes your check, then you have a right to that appraisal. It is now yours because you have paid for it.

The Verification Process

How much information the lender will need to verify depends on the loan program you have chosen, the loan size, how much equity is in your home you are using as collateral (also known as loan-to-value), and how good your credit is. If you are fortunate and your loan has been marked for a streamlined underwriting process, which means no verifications are required, the lender might be able to get your loan to the closing table either that afternoon or within a couple of days. If the loan is not streamlined, then the lender reviewing your loan application will need to verify a few things. Among the things that the lender will need to verify is your record for paying your first mortgage loan. Most of the time the mortgage pay history can be found in your credit bureau report. The lender will then need to verify the payoff amounts of any consumer loan you intend to pay off with this second mortgage loan.

The lender will also be reviewing the income documents you have provided in order to verify that your debt-to-income ratio meets guidelines. The debt-to-income ratio takes the monthly payment amount of all the loans (not being consolidated) that you owe (not including utility bills) plus the proposed monthly payment of this loan and divides that number by your verified gross monthly income. The acceptable debt-to-income ratio varies with each lending institution and ranges from thirty-six percent to fifty percent. **A debt-to-income ratio below thirty percent is much better than one over forty percent.** There are potentially five other tasks that the lender may be required to perform prior to final approval. The following could be required:

An appraisal, or a less expensive market analysis, will be performed on the property being used as collateral for the loan. The purpose of the appraisal, or market analysis, is to determine a value for the collateral in order to calculate the loan-to-value ratio. (The loan-to-value ratio is the current principle balance of your first mortgage plus the proposed loan amount of the new second mortgage divided by the value of the collateral.) The lender will generally have three options on how to verify the value of the home. The lender may require that a full appraisal be performed on the property. The appraisal method is the most time consuming and the most costly option. The report can take from three days to two full weeks to complete and will typically costs between two hundred and fifty to three hundred and fifty dollars. An appraisal is a report that compares the property being used as collateral to three other similar sized homes that have recently sold in the same general vicinity. This report should be performed by a fully licensed and state certified appraiser. A second option for the lender is to use a less expensive home value report or market analysis report from a research company. This report can be completed in a matter of an hour to two days depending on how much detail is required. Typically, the cost for this report is less than one hundred dollars. The third option, and the least expensive, is for the lender to simply use the real estate tax assessed value of your property as determined by the county or city you live in.

The mortgage company will perform a flood search on the actual physical location of your house. The flood search is a federal requirement on all mortgage loan transactions where a structure is involved. The purpose of the report is to check to see if the house being used as collateral is located in a flood zone. If the home is in a designated flood plain, then you will have to buy flood insurance. The flood insurance premium can be very expensive. It is necessary to have flood insurance because the standard homeowner's insurance policy will not insure your house against any damage caused by a flood.

Either a title search company or a local attorney will perform a title search on the property at the local courthouse where the property is located. The purpose of the title search is to check and make sure that you are the legal owners. The search will also verify that there are no other liens, judgments, or encumbrances that might jeopardize the lien position of the home equity loan. Some lenders may require title insurance to accompany the title search. Title insurance guarantees the lien position and protects you in case any errors or omissions are later found. Title insurance is not mandatory for a second mortgage loan unless the lending company requires it. I would not recommend that you request title insurance yourself because you should have gotten the insurance when you bought the property. If you did not get title insurance when you originally purchased the property, then it might be a good idea to get it now.

You will have to provide proof of homeowner's insurance to the lender before you close on your home equity loan. This is a good time to review your homeowner's policy to make sure that you have adequate coverage and that the policy includes "replacement cost". Replacement cost means that if your house is damaged or destroyed, that it will be repaired using *today's* cost (i.e., what it would take to rebuild the house in today's market) not what it cost to originally build.

The lender may require verification of your employment. In most cases, supplying the lender with a copy of your most recent paycheck can satisfy this requirement. If not, you will need to provide the lender with a manager's or supervisor's name and a work telephone number so the verification process can be completed verbally over the phone.

Credit Insurance

A popular product with second mortgages is credit insurance or payment protection. **Credit insurance cannot be required in order to be approved for a home equity loan.** The monthly insurance premiums associated with the credit insurance are generally more costly when compared to the amount of money you are borrowing and what is available through independent insurance companies. Most people will have adequate coverage through their employer or through an independent third party insurance provider. Not all credit insurance options mentioned are available in all states. Also, the policies will generally have restrictions and maximum benefits that might not fully cover your loan. So you need to be careful and read the fine print. **Be aware that each insurance product that you select will add *an extra cost* to your monthly payment**.

There are three basic types of credit insurance policies that you could possibly get with your second mortgage loan and they are: credit life, disability or accidental and health, and involuntary unemployment insurance. Credit life insurance is life insurance that pays only on the balance remaining on your loan that is owed to the creditor should you become deceased. It is called decreasing term coverage. **The insurance only covers the amount that you owe on the loan and your estate does not receive any extra money.** Most people will have adequate life insurance coverage through a regular life insurance policy by either his or her employer and/or through an independent insurance company that will pay *your estate* a much larger lump sum payment upon your death that should cover *all* your debts and obligations.

Disability insurance, also known as accidental and health insurance, will cover the monthly payment of the loan for as long as you are unable to return to work and until the loan is paid off due to an injury or illness. Typically, you need to be out of work for either fifteen or thirty days until the insurance will begin paying the monthly payment. The disability insurance covers only the monthly payment associated with the loan and does not cover any of your other debts or loans. If you have disability insurance through your employer, then you need to verify when the benefits will start paying if you are out of work. Sometimes the disability or accidental and health policy through your employer will not start paying you until you have been out of work for sixty or ninety days. If that is the case, and you do not have adequate cash reserves, then you might want to consider getting the disability coverage. Most people will have adequate coverage through their employer or an independent insurance company that will pay you a percentage of your lost wages.

A third type of payment protection that the lender may offer you is involuntary unemployment insurance. This insurance pays your monthly payment after you have been laid off from your current job for at least thirty days. Depending on the industry, the company you work for, and the amount of cash reserves or investments you have available, this might be a good policy to get on your loan. This insurance will only cover the monthly payment associated with this loan and the policy will usually have a term restriction on how many months the insurance will pay. And remember you cannot be required to get credit insurance, or payment protection, as a requirement for being approved for a loan.

Chapter 7: Ready to Close the Loan

The loan is ready to be closed when the information from your loan application has been verified and all necessary reports have been completed. In most cases, you will be closing the loan with the original lender, who took the loan application at the beginning of the process, in his or her office. Or you could be receiving the closing loan package in the mail if you went through an internet service or a through the mail application. In any event, **you should go over the final figures with the lender prior to going to the closing table.** This review prevents there from being any surprises or last minute changes. If there are any changes, you will want to take care of them before you get to the closing table. **If there are any surprises, or if you uncover anything that you do not agree with, DO NOT SIGN the paperwork.**

When reviewing the paperwork, pay close attention to the final Settlement Statement. **Make sure all charges and fees listed are very close to what you agreed to when you applied for the loan.** You can do this by comparing the charges listed on the final Settlement Statement with the estimated closing cost listed in the Good Faith Estimate that you received when you applied for the loan. It is also important to review the Final Truth in Lending Statement (the promissory note). You should check this form to make sure the total monthly payment is what you were expecting. This form should also indicate when the first payment is due. Remember, in most cases, **it is a good idea to have your second mortgage payment due at least fifteen days after your first mortgage payment is due if you get paid two or more times a month.** Lastly, check the Deed of Trust to make sure that your name is properly spelled and that the property has been correctly identified.

As a safeguard, because you are placing a second mortgage lien on your

primary residence, this loan will have a three-day rescission period. This means that you have three business days to cancel the transaction at no cost to you, except for maybe the appraisal fee that was discussed earlier. The three-day rescission period is called a "cooling off period". This allows you time to review the loan documents thoroughly at your home without any sale pressures. After the three days have expired, the loan will be disbursed, and you will then be able to pick up your loan proceeds check. If your are placing a lien on a secondary residence or investment property, there will be no rescission period so you will want to make sure that everything in the loan is as promised prior to signing.

Congratulations!

Section IV:
The Consumer Loan

Introduction

Consumer loans are an everyday part of borrowing money. In today's lending environment, loan approval can take as little as fifteen minutes. A lot of the time, you can get the money that you need on the same day that you applied for the loan. Consumer loans come in many different forms, such as an installment loan for financing the purchase of a new car at the dealership. Another form is an in-store charge card for financing the purchase of a new living room set. It could be in the form of a credit card used to pay for dinner at the local family restaurant. A consumer loan could also be in the form of a personal loan (for any reason) from you local financial source. This section will explore the following: The benefits and drawbacks of the three main types of consumer loans, the situations for which each type of loan should be used, the other products that are available with a consumer loan, and the application process.

Chapter 1: What Type of Consumer Loan is Right for Me?

There are basically three types of consumer loans that you need to understand: The Installment Loan, the Line of Credit and the Demand Note. Every bank or financial lending institution has their own name for these products, but they are all basically the same. Each type of loan is specifically designed to meet a particular borrowing need. Understanding what each type of loan is, when it should be used, and how to repay the debt will help you to better manage your money and credit.

The Installment Loan

The Installment Loan is the first type of consumer loan to be discussed. This type of loan is primarily used when you are financing a one-time, large purchase or you need the money for a one-time, isolated event. A one-time, large purchase could be to buy a car, a new computer, new windows or a new roof for the house, or even a new dining room set. A one-time, isolated event could be to consolidate your student loans after college, a major repair bill, a wedding, or a small consolidation loan for up to ten thousand dollars. If you are a homeowner in need of a larger consolidation loan, please review Section Three on Home Equity Loans.

There are many benefits to the Installment Loan. One benefit is that each loan is for a unique purpose, which can help you to manage and budget your payments. You will be able to determine exactly what each loan costs. Another benefit with the Installment Loan is that the *terms are fixed*. The interest rate and monthly payment stays the same throughout the duration of the loan. This helps you to plan your monthly family budget to ensure that the loan is repaid on time. This is very beneficial if you are on a limited or fixed income. However, a drawback is that each time you need money, you will have to reapply for a new loan. Nowadays, that is not much of a hindrance because the process of borrowing money for an installment loan is very quick and efficient. Sometimes you can close the loan and get the money within an hour to two.

The interest rate and terms of the Installment Loan will vary depending on several factors such as how much money you need to borrow, if there is any collateral for the loan, and how good your credit score and overall credit history is. The typical Installment Loan will have a repayment term anywhere from twelve to sixty months. The interest rate will vary greatly depending on the collateral pledged. **The more similar the collateral for the loan is to cash, the lower the interest rate will be.** Pledging a certificate of deposit (commonly known as a CD) will get you the lowest interest rate available and a much lower rate than offering the title to a two-year-old automobile. That same two-year-old automobile will get you a lower rate than a loan with *no* collateral, called an unsecured loan.

The Line of Credit

The second type of consumer loan is the Line of Credit. The Line of Credit is a commitment made by a bank or financial institution to extend an open invitation for you to borrow money in the future up to a predetermined (credit) limit. You would borrow money from the "account" by getting a cash advance, writing a check, or using a credit card specifically tied to that line of credit. You would not need to reapply for a loan every time you needed to borrow money from this loan because it is designed for *continuous usage*. The most popular Line of Credit products are: the Home Equity Line of Credit (please refer to Section Three, Chapter Four), the Credit Card, the In-Store Charge Card (also known as the Department Store Charge Card), or the Unsecured Line of Credit. The Line of Credit Loan is best suited for people who are financially responsible and plan to make a number of purchases in the near future for which paying by cash or check is not an option.

The main benefit of this type of loan is that it is open-ended. Any time that you need money you can access cash, up to the credit line limit, in a variety of ways. If you plan to use your line of credit at retail stores or for online shopping, then you will need to get a credit card. If you plan to take cash advances, then you will need to get a home equity line of credit or an unsecured personal line of credit. The reason is that most credit cards will charge a fee for cash advances and lines of credit will not.

The interest rate and terms of the Line of Credit will vary greatly. The Line of Credit can have either a fixed interest rate or a variable interest rate. Most Lines of Credit, if they are variable interest rate loans, will be tied to the U.S. prime rate or the LIBOR rate. As the prime rate or LIBOR rate changes, your interest rate will change. The Line of Credit typically does not have a fixed monthly payment. The monthly payment will vary depending on what the average monthly balance is from the previous month. Most Lines of Credit have a minimum monthly repayment amount between one percent and three percent of the average outstanding loan balance.

A drawback is that the rate and terms *can be changed* at any time by the lender, as stated in your Line of Credit Agreement. Most companies with which you have an open line of credit will check your credit report periodically to verify that your *overall* credit is still in good standing and all of your debts are being repaid as agreed. If your credit score or overall credit deteriorates, the terms and interest rate can be changed by the lender. If, during one of these routine credit reviews, the financial institution notices that your credit rating (score) is below a certain threshold, your credit line can be lowered or closed. If you go into default or become late with your monthly payment, the creditor can also increase your interest rate substantially to a predetermined default rate.

The Demand Note

The third type of consumer loan is the Demand Note. The Demand Note is a short-term loan for the purpose of using the cash now and then repaying the loan in full with a lump sum repayment in the very near future. This loan is generally borrowed for a thirty-day, ninety-day or a six-month period with no scheduled monthly payments in-between. When the loan matures, the total amount borrowed (the principle amount) plus the accrued interest is due and payable in full. The Demand Loan can be secured or unsecured and the interest rate can be fixed or variable. As with the other two types of loans, the more similar the collateral is to cash, the lower the interest rate will be. The main benefit to the Demand Loan is that you can satisfy your immediate need for money without a long-term commitment.

Examples of situations when this type of consumer loan is best suited are:

- You know that you will be getting a large commission or bonus check and you found a very good deal on a new car that just can't wait.
- You will be receiving an inheritance check in the very near future, but a family member is in need of some financial assistance now.
- You have encountered a very good business opportunity and you need the cash now, but it will take a couple of weeks to liquidate an investment.

The Bridge Loan

Another instance when borrowers find the Demand Note very beneficial is as a Bridge Loan. A Bridge Loan allows you to buy a new residence before your old home sells by "bridging" the equity of the two properties together. The Bridge Loan is typically a six or twelve month loan that lets you cash out the equity in the house that is for sale (your existing residence) so that you can put a larger down payment on the new house you are hoping to purchase. This allows you to borrow less on the property you are buying, thereby lowering your new mortgage payment. A lien is placed on either the house for sale or both the house for sale and the house being purchased. The lien placement is determined by how much equity is available in the house you are selling and how much down payment money is needed for the house you hope to buy.

As an example of a Bridge Loan, let's say that you are selling your current residence for $160,000 and you only owe $75,000 on it. The house you are hoping to buy costs $200,000. You want to borrow enough money to put 20% cash down and avoid paying mortgage insurance (PMI). You would get a Bridge Loan for $50,000 secured as a second lien on the house that is for sale to cover the down payment, closing costs, and moving expenses.

$200,000	Purchase Price	$160,000	Selling Price, Old Residence
x 20%	Down Pmt. Ratio	x 80%	Loan-to-value Threshold
$40,000	Required Down Pmt.	128,000	Available Equity
		-75,000	First Mortgage Balance
		$53,000	Available Equity

Of the $50,000 Bridge Loan, $40,000 would go to cover the twenty-percent down payment requirement. Then approximately $3,000 to $5,000 (allow approximately

2% for closing cost) would be used to cover any closing costs associated with the purchase, and the rest of the money would go into your checking or savings account to cover any other miscellaneous moving expenses. The loan would be for a six-month term with no monthly payment in-between. When you sell your old residence, the $50,000 Bridge Loan, plus the accrued interest, would be paid off along with the first mortgage loan of $75,000.

One drawback to this type of loan is if your house does not sell within the six or twelve-month time period as anticipated and the bridge loan matures. The lender can do one of two things. Some lenders will let you modify (extend) the loan term for another six or twelve month period, while other lenders may require that the loan be "termed out" as a regular Home Equity Loan (as discussed in Section Three) with regularly scheduled monthly payments. Therefore, you need to be careful and understand the housing market in your area to feel fairly confident that your house will sell in the allotted time frame and that you can afford the potential second mortgage payment if it doesn't sell.

The second drawback to the Bridge Loan is that if your house does not sell for the listed sales price, but sells for less instead, you could be left with a shortfall. That means that you would owe more money on the house than what you are able to sell it for. With a Bridge Loan, you need to have a contingency plan in place in case this happens. There are generally four options available to cover the difference: (1) Bring cash to the closing table, (2) liquidate an investment, (3) obtain an unsecured loan, or (4) transfer the remaining balance to a second mortgage loan secured to the new residence.

Chapter 2: Understanding the Consumer Loan Process

The process of borrowing money by obtaining a consumer loan is very easy in today's lending environment because of certain technological advancements in the field. Most financial institutions can approve and close the average consumer loan (the Installment Loan or the Line of Credit Loan) within one to two hours due to streamlined loan application software programs, online instant credit bureau reports, and computer generated credit-scoring models. However, the Bridge Loan or the Home Equity Line of Credit could take a couple of days or a couple of weeks to close depending on the collateral and the amount of money being borrowed. There are a couple of steps that you can take prior to contacting a lender or filling out an application that will make the process go more smoothly and proceed with greater efficiency.

Determining Your Income

The first thing you need to be able to prove is how much income you make. In order to properly answer that question, you should look at your paycheck to see exactly how much your gross income is. The gross income is the amount of money you have earned prior to any deductions for things such as taxes, insurances, and retirement. If you are an hourly employee, determine what your hourly pay rate is, excluding any overtime pay. If you are a salary employee, verify how much your income is with each paycheck. If you are a commission employee or receive large bonuses, then you need to calculate how much you have *averaged* over the last one to two years, you can not just present your best month.

In order to use the extra income from overtime or commissions, you need to be able to prove that you have consistently received that money over a period of at least the last two years. It is best to have your most recent paycheck stub and the last year of your W-2 form readily available when you apply for the loan. **However, it is not a good idea to use any overtime or bonus income to qualify for a loan. It is also not a good idea to base your family budget on this extra income.** When the overtime is stopped or the bonus income is gone, you might not be able to afford your present debt load or your current standard of living. This could have a damaging effect on your credit rating and the credit score that you have worked so hard to build.

If you are self-employed, then you need to have copies of the last two years of your complete tax returns, along with all the schedules, for both individual and business, if applicable. Depending on the type of loan for which you are applying, the size of the loan, and the type of collateral, the lender may ask for proof of income. The self-employed borrowers who are successful in obtaining a loan are generally the ones who disclose their true income. If you are self-employed and do not report all of your income, then you might have a harder time getting approved for a loan if the lender requires proof of income. If that is the case, then you should be able to provide documents to support your income claims. The best alternative, when the tax returns will not work, is to have the last six to twelve months of bank statements available, along with a simple Profit and Loss Statement for your business.

By law, you cannot be discriminated against for the type of income you receive such as alimony, child support, social security, disability, etc. **The key is being able to verify that the income you are receiving and using to qualify for the loan will be consistently received by you on a *regular* and *ongoing* basis**. You should never let your income discourage you from applying for a loan. It is always best to apply for the loan, provide proof of your income if required, and let the bank or lending company determine how much income is verifiable and can be used with the loan.

Reviewing Your Credit

The second thing that you need to be knowledgeable about is your credit history. You need to be honest with the lender, especially if you have any derogatory credit references (such as a bankruptcy, judgment, or collection activity) within the last seven years or periods of late payments within the last couple of years. If you are a cosigner on any loan, verify with the financial institution that the loan you cosigned for is being repaid on time and is up to date and current. If you are a divorced person whose ex-spouse did not make payments on joint debts as agreed, or if you have filed for bankruptcy, or if you have medical collections, or have been laid off from work for a period of time, you need to discuss these life changing events with your lender. It is better to be honest with the lender and have your responses prepared ahead of time. Most of the time, during the credit investigation, the lender will uncover any credit deficiencies. Your failure to disclose any past or present credit problems in advance will only slow the process or possibly cause your loan application to be declined.

Determining Your Net Worth

The third thing that you should do is to determine your estimated net worth. To arrive at this figure, you should list the assets you own (real estate, cars, etc.) and estimate their worth. Have in hand the current values of your investment accounts (retirement plan, 410K, stock portfolio, etc.) and be able to list with whom they are held. These assets can act as a secondary repayment source in case your primary repayment source, usually your regular paycheck, is interrupted or terminated.

Depending on the type of loan you are requesting and your credit standing, the assets that you own can be very important in helping to get an approval for a loan in spite of your otherwise marginal credit rating.

Applying for the Loan

The final step is to complete a credit application. In today's business environment, there are numerous ways to apply for a consumer loan. You can apply in person, over the phone, at a retail store, using the internet, or through the mail. If you are going to apply in person at a bank or lending institution, it is best to contact the lender by phone to make an appointment so that he or she can scheduled a block of uninterrupted time for the two of you to meet. If you complete an application over the phone or the internet, it is important that the company you are applying with is a reputable lender because you are volunteering very valuable information about yourself, such as your social security number and date of birth. If you are applying with a local company over the phone, you can check the local chapter of the Better Business Bureau or ask for references. If you are applying over the Internet, you can check for news articles about the company or view the company's public information at a number of financial web sites. If you are not comfortable applying in these manners, then have the company mail you an application.

No matter how you apply, you must eventually sign a promissory note that makes you contractually obligated to repay the debt as agreed. Some applications, such as credit cards or in-store department charge cards, have this feature included with the application. **Be sure to read the fine print and ask the lender to explain anything that is unclear to you about the terms or language on the application form *before* you sign.** You must be sure that you *understand* the answers to the questions. Some good questions to ask are as follows:

- What is the annual percentage rate?

- What is the payment due date?

- Is the interest rate a fixed or variable rate?

- Is there an annual fee?

- How is the minimum monthly payment determined?

Chapter 3: Other Consumer Loan Associated Products

The Cash Option

A popular incentive that is frequently offered with a consumer loan is the cash option. You might recognize the popular phrase "six-months same as cash". A cash option is a sales promotion offered by a business that helps it to sell large ticket merchandise or service contracts. Typically, cash option periods last ninety-days, six months, or twelve months. This type of option can be available on both installment loans and lines of credit. The cash option period means that you have a certain amount of time (ninety-days, six months, or twelve months) to pay off the loan *interest free*.

As an example, suppose you purchased a $2,500 bedroom set. The contract that you signed says that you have agreed to finance the purchase for thirty-six months on an installment loan basis at 18% with a "twelve-month same as cash option". That means that you have twelve months, or 365 days, from the date of purchase, to pay $2,500 to the creditor without paying any interest (interest free). Looking at an amortization schedule, if you pay off the loan within the twelve month cash option period, you would save $754.00 in finance charges (interest).

The advantage of using the cash option is to save money in finance charges by paying off the loan during the cash option period. **It is best to pay or mail the payment at least two or three weeks *prior to* the cash option expiration date.** This will allow extra time in case the payment is lost in the mail or the company is late crediting your loan. If you do not have the cash available to payoff the loan in full, then pay as much as you can and refinance the remaining portion with another lender. That will allow you to pay off the original loan interest free. The new loan would then *start* accruing interest from the point of the new loan forward, instead of from the date of purchase (twelve months prior). In the example above, that would have saved you at least $395.00 in finance charges that had accumulated over the first twelve months of the loan.

After the cash option period expires, the lender will not allow another cash option period (interest free period) on the original purchase (loan amount). **If you keep the original cash option loan open and begin to make regular monthly payments after the cash option period has expired, then you might be required to pay *all* the accrued interest from the time the loan was originally opened.** The accrued interest can be a substantial amount depending on the size of the loan.

As the customer, you need to make sure that the cash option program is detailed in the actual loan contract. **You will want to have *in writing* the exact date the cash option period expires and how the accrued interest will be handled.** Some consumer loans will have a "true" cash option period. That means that the interest on the loan will not actually start accruing until the day *after* the cash option period has ended. If that is the case, then you would not have to get another loan (unless you can get a better interest rate). Most cash option loans will require you to pay the interest owed from the date of purchase. **As the customer (borrower), the key**

is to understand the terms of the cash option and when the interest will start accruing.

The Cash Rebate

A second popular incentive to get customers to apply for a consumer loan is the cash rebate. The cash rebate is mainly offered with new car financing as an enticement for people to buy new cars. The competition between automakers has become very intense and the cash rebates can be substantial. There are primarily three options to choose from when you are offered a large cash rebate. Your financial situation and net worth will determine which of the three options is available to you and is best suited for you.

To illustrate how a cash rebate works, let's say that you have found a new vehicle that you'd like to buy priced at $20,000. The dealership is promoting a cash rebate of $2,000, if you pay cash for the new vehicle or zero percent financing for thirty-six months. There are three options to choose from: (1) Pay cash for the car and get the cash rebate, (2) finance the car at zero percent for 36 months, or (3) obtain a loan elsewhere and get the cash rebate from the dealership. How are you going to know which option to choose? In order to choose the best option, you need to be able to determine what the *total cost* will actually be for each of them and figure out which one fits best given your present financial and credit position.

Option one is to pay cash for the vehicle. You could pay the dealership $20,000 cash for the car and get $2,000 cash back. With this option, the most important consideration is what the $20,000 would have earned for you had it been invested for three years earning an appropriate rate of return. To calculate this, you would look at a Future Value Table. (You can find a Future Value Table at a number of financial websites that offer investment services.) The table indicates that investing $20,000 for 36 months at a 6% compounded average return rate would generate approximately $3,950 in interest income. Therefore, the total cost of the vehicle calculated by choosing option one will be $21,950. The $21,950 breaks down as follows: $20,000 cash paid for the car, plus $3,950 in lost interest income, minus the $2,000 cash rebate. (This option is only available if you can come up with $20,000 in cash.)

$20,000 Purchase Price	$20,000 Purchase Price
x 6% Rate of Return	+3,950 Loss Interest Income
$3,950 Interest Income	-2,000 Cash Rebate
	$21,950 Total Cost of Purchase

Option two is to finance the vehicle at zero percent. You could finance the new automobile through the dealership at zero percent interest for the term established by the dealership, usually thirty-six or sixty months. The total cost for the car under the zero percent interest option would be $20,000. If you could afford Option One, but choose to invest the $20,000 instead, then the actual cost to purchase to automobile would only be $18,050.

$20,000 Purchase Price	$20,000 Purchase Price
0.00 No Cash Rebate	+2,000 Loss of Cash Rebate
0.00 Lack of earned interest	-3,950 Earned Interest Income
$20,000 Total Cost Purchase	$18,050 Total Cost of Purchase

Option three is to finance the loan elsewhere. Using this option, you would pay cash to the dealership in order to collect the cash rebate, but you would actually get financing for the automobile elsewhere. Let's suppose that you call your bank and learn that their current new automobile interest rate for 36 months to finance $18,000 ($20,000 - $2,000 rebate) is 7%. Looking at an amortization table, it shows the total repayment of the loan to be $20,050. Therefore, the total cost to purchase the car using Option Three is $20,050.

$20,000 Purchase Price
-2,000 Cash Rebate
+2,050 Finance Charge, 7% for 36 mo.
$20,050 Total Cost of Purchase

Keep in mind that not all of these options will necessarily be available to you depending on your current financial and credit situation. For instance, qualifying for a zero percent financing loan requires a very good credit score and a clean credit report.

Perhaps you are still wondering which option is the best. If you have the twenty thousand dollars of cash available, then the best option for you would be Option two, provided that the cash you had available to purchase the automobile was properly invested. If only options two and three were available to you because you did not have the cash, the cost difference between those two options is only $50 ($20,000 versus $20,050) in this example. Option three might prove to be a slightly better choice if you were to invest the cash rebate wisely or use it to payoff one of your current high rate consumer loans, possibly a credit card with an interest rate of 18% or 21%.

As a homeowner, choosing Option three would be best if you had enough equity in your house in order to get a home equity loan to finance the auto purchase (refer to Section Three on Home Equity Loans). That is because home equity loans typically have a lower interest rate than an auto secured consumer loan. For example, the interest rate being offered on a home equity loan could be about 4.50%. That makes the total cost to purchase the automobile $19,300. In addition, the interest paid on a home equity loan is potentially tax deductible, thus lowering the total cost to purchase even more.

> $20,000 Purchase Price
> -2,000 Cash Rebate
> +1,300 Finance Charge,4.5%for 36mo.
> $19,300 Total Cost of Purchase

The key to deciding which option to take, either two or three, is to look at *the* total cost of purchase.** *If you are a homeowner with equity in your house or you could get a low enough interest rate, then option three would be best.

Simple Interest vs. Rule of 78's

There are two ways interest is calculated for Installment Loans. Interest is calculated using Simple Interest or the Rule of 78's. The difference between the two methods is how the interest is calculated and repaid. The simple interest method is the most widely used method among lending institutions. Simple interest means that the interest is computed on the present principle loan balance without compounding. As the borrower, you are paying interest (finance charges) on the actual principle loan balance. The interest is more evenly spread out over the term of the loan. If you pay the loan off early, prior to the maturity date, you are not penalized by incurring extra finance charges. **This is the preferred method if you pay your loans off early or refinance them frequently.** As an example, let's say you borrowed $1,000 at 10% for 1 year. The interest for the first month is $8.33 (10% ÷ 12 months X $1,000).

The Rule of 78's (also know as the Sum of the Digits) method is a mathematical formula used to calculate interest owed when a loan is paid off early and the interest is pre-computed using the "Add-on" interest method. The interest is not as evenly distributed throughout the term of the loan as with Simple Interest. You pay the majority of interest during the beginning third of the loan. If the loan is paid off early it will cost you more money in finance charges (interest) than the simple interest method.

The Rule of 78's calculates the interest owed when a borrower pays off the loan prior to its maturity date. The formula for calculating the interest owed starts by adding up the sum of the number of months for which the loan payments are scheduled. For a twelve month loan, the total is 78 (1+2+3+4.....+12= 78). This number is then divided by the month that the loan was paid off, starting backward. As an example, let's say you have a $1,000 loan for 12 months at 10%. (The monthly payment is $91.67.) If you paid off the loan in the first month, then the interest (finance charge) owed is $14.10 (12/78 X $91.67). This $1,000 loan would have cost you $5.77 ($14.10 - $8.33) more that the Simple Interest Loan if the loans were paid off in the first month.

The Rule of 78's method is only beneficial if you do not pay your loans off early or refinance them. Some lending companies will offer you a lower interest rate but will use the Rule of 78's method to recoup the interest loss to offset offering a lower interest rate. The company lending the money at a slightly cheaper rate, using the Rule of 78's method, is gambling that you will pay the loan off early or refinance it. That way they will actually make a little more money on the loan as compared to the competitor who was offering a slightly higher interest rate, but using the simple interest method to calculate the finance charges.

Credit Insurance

Another popular product with consumer loans is credit insurance or payment protection. **Credit insurance cannot be required in order to be approved for a consumer loan**. The monthly insurance premiums associated with credit insurance are generally more costly when compared to the amount of money you are borrowing and what is available through independent insurance companies. Most people will have adequate coverage through their employer or through an independent third party insurance provider. Not all credit insurance options mentioned are available in all states and for all loans. Also, the policies will generally have restrictions and maximum benefits that might not fully cover your loan. So you need to be careful and read the fine print. **Be aware that each insurance you select will add an *extra cost* to your monthly payment.**

There are four basic types of credit insurance policies that you could possibly get with a consumer loan and they are: credit life, disability or accidental and health, involuntary unemployment insurance, and personal property insurance. Credit life insurance is life insurance that pays only on the balance remaining on your loan that is owed to the creditor. It is called "decreasing term coverage". **The insurance only covers the amount that you owe on the loan and your estate does not receive any extra money.** Most people will have adequate life insurance coverage through a regular life insurance policy by either his or her employer and/or through an independent insurance company that will pay your estate a lump sum payment upon your death that could be used towards *all* your debts and obligations.

Disability insurance, also known as accidental and health insurance, will cover the monthly payment of the loan for as long as you are unable to return to work and until the loan is paid off due to an injury or illness. Typically, you need to be out of work for either fifteen or thirty days before the insurance will begin paying the monthly payment. **The disability insurance covers only the monthly payment associated with the loan and does not cover any of your other debts or loans.** If you have disability insurance through your employer, then you need to verify when the benefits will start paying if you are caused to be out of work. Sometimes the disability or accidental and health policy through your employer will not start paying until you have been out of work for sixty or ninety days. If that is the case, and you do not have adequate cash reserves, then you might want to consider getting the disability coverage. Most people will have adequate coverage through their employer or an independent insurance company that will directly pay you a percentage of your lost wages.

A third type of payment protection that the lender might offer you is involuntary unemployment insurance. This insurance covers your monthly payment after you have been laid off from you current job for at least thirty days. Depending on the industry (such as textile or mining) and the company you work for, and the amount of cash reserves or investments you have available, this might be a good policy to get on your loan. Remember though, this insurance will only cover the monthly payment associated with *this* loan and the policy will usually have a term restriction on how many months the insurance will pay.

The fourth type of credit insurance is personal property insurance. This insurance is typically used when you are pledging household items as collateral for an installment loan. You will not need this coverage if you have homeowner's insurance, renter's insurance, or you still live with your parents (your belongings are insured under your parent's policy). **This policy will only cover any damage to the collateral being pledged.** Any insurance claim that is filed, the money is applied to the principle balance of the loan. I recommend that you do not get this coverage. If you rent and do not have any insurance coverage on your personal belongings, then you should get a basic renter's insurance policy with replacement cost to cover *all* of your possessions.

Chapter 4: Closing the Loan

Now you have been approved for the loan and are ready to sign the promissory note or loan contract. Make sure you have read the agreement and ask any questions *prior to* signing the note. **Once you sign the note, you are contractually obligated for that debt with the stated terms.** Make sure the monthly payment and interest rate is what you discussed and the due date works well with your family budget. **If you have any type of payment protection or credit insurance on the loan, make sure it is what *you wanted (and requested)* and not what the lender "placed" on your loan.** Remember that the lender cannot require you to have any credit or payment protection on the loan as a condition of the approval. Depending on the type of collateral used for the loan there may be some fees associated with it. Make sure all fees and the total cost of the loan have been properly disclosed and explained to you *prior to* signing any agreement.

You have just successfully secured the right consumer loan product at the right rate. This is a process you will repeat many times during your borrowing money life. Each time you go through the loan approval process, you become a more experienced and savvier borrower. The best advice is to shop around for the right rate and terms that best meet *your* financial needs and fits well in your family budget.

Congratulations!

Section V
The Five Most Common Credit Issues

Introduction

The key to good credit is that it is earned over time. Your credit rating is derived from a complicated formula produced by a computer program that relies on facts and information to determine your credit risk. Therefore, the credit score is *unbiased* and *non-prejudiced*. It takes good family budgeting and financial discipline to maintain a good credit rating. In today's borrowing environment, this is very important because your credit rating can be quickly compromised or damaged as the result of helping others or being caught unprepared for a life-changing event.

Section Five concerns the five most common credit issues that I have found to be the most unclear in today's borrowing environment. At some point in your borrowing money life, you will probably experience at least two of these five credit issues: (1) Establishing credit (2) cosigning for credit (3) divorcing and its affects on your credit (4) overcoming credit problems by reestablishing credit and (5) surviving a bankruptcy. This section describes each scenario individually and in-depth, giving you recommendations about how to handle each unique situation.

Chapter 1: Establishing Credit

Some people will say that trying to establish credit is almost an impossible task. For a young person, the first attempts at establishing credit can be very difficult and frustrating. It takes time and patience. Nobody is born with credit, so everyone has to start somewhere. **A good credit score is something that you develop over time using good budgeting and bill paying habits.** Establishing credit for yourself is a lot easier if you have a parent or guardian who is willing to cosign for the first couple of consumer loans to get you started, although a cosigner is not mandatory to establish credit. However, before you can begin to establish credit, you must be old enough to enter into a legally binding contract. In most states, that means that you must be at least eighteen years of age or older.

After graduating from high school or college, most young people will enter the work force either as a full-time or part-time employee. Whatever you do, one of the most important things to remember is that **your debts and bills must be paid when they are due**. If a company reports a delinquency on newly established credit, it will inhibit your ability to easily borrow money or obtain new credit in the immediate future. In addition, **delinquencies most often subject you to *higher* interest rates and fees.** Even the very first bills that are in your name, like the phone or electric, must be paid on time! It is always best to get started on the right foot in regard to credit. **A key point to remember is that establishing good credit is something that has to be earned; it cannot simply be given to you.**

The first thing to do when establishing credit is to open a checking account at a local bank branch. A young person could open an account at the bank of his or her parent's or guardian's. A person could call around to find out which bank offers a basic checking account plan with minimal or no fees. Some consideration should be given ahead of time as to what services are important to have. Such services might include: Direct deposit of paychecks, an ATM card to be used at money machines (convenient to where you live and work), a debit card, and overdraft protection services. These features make depositing, accessing, and controlling money very easy and convenient. If you are going to college or work out of town, you will want to open your checking account in the town where you will be spending the most time. Another option is to do some research to find out what banks have branches and ATM machines in both locations.

Most customers can benefit from an overdraft account. **An overdraft account is a line of credit that is attached to your checking account.** It is designed to protect you in case you write a check for which there are not sufficient funds (money) in the checking account to cover the check or it can be used to borrow a small amount of money to cover an unforeseen bill. An overdraft account should not be an excuse *not* to balance your checking account on a regular basis. **Its main purpose is to protect you from bouncing checks and incurring fees due to an *oversight* or an addition or subtraction error.** The overdraft account is a consumer loan on which you will pay interest for any outstanding balance owed. Most banks will approve you for their minimum overdraft protection line. Check the bank with which you are opening your checking account in order to confirm that it will report this overdraft account as a credit reference for you to one of the major credit reporting agencies. Most midsize and large banks report this type of credit appropriately, but some smaller, local banks will not.

The second thing to do is to get a credit card (see Section Four, Chapter One). The first place to inquire is the local bank branch where you have just opened your new checking account. However, you can also inquire with any other financial institution because there are many places that offer credit cards. Beware of the costs involved with a credit card and make sure that you read and understand the fine print. Some credit cards have annual fees, some have high interest rates, and some cards will require a cash deposit. If you are fortunate enough to have a parent or guardian who will cosign for you, then you should be able to get a low-interest, unsecured major credit card. Begin to use this card slowly for purchases that will cost no more than what you can afford to pay off at the end of the month. When you receive your monthly statement, promptly pay the credit card balance *in full.* **Remember that the key is to establish a good payment history and to have that good pay history** *reported* **to a major credit bureau.** Try to maintain your good payment habit for six months before applying for another type of consumer loan. This allows you time to get an understanding of how the credit process works and familiarizes you with budgeting in the payments. Many new borrowers make the mistake of charging more than they can payoff in a couple of months. Since interest is added monthly to the balance, this type of credit situation can quickly snowball into a situation wherein the person is not able to afford the minimum monthly payment causing their credit score to suffer.

The third thing you should do is to get a local gas charge card and/or department (or clothing) store card. Use the charge card regularly when you are purchasing anything from that particular store. Or use the gas card regularly to purchase gas at your favorite gas station or convenient store. When you receive your monthly bill, promptly pay it off. Again, the goal is to establish a good repayment history... not to run up the debt. Incidentally, by paying off your balances monthly before the due date, you avoid paying finance charges.

As you start to build credit and open these first couple of new accounts over the next twelve months, **it is important that you do not inquire at multiple places for credit.** You need to be disciplined in your approach and choose the companies you want to do business with wisely. Making six to twelve inquiries for credit over a three to six month period of time will have a detrimental effect. This is because it has a negative effect on your credit score and might raise suspicion with underwriters about what credit you actually have open.

A fourth thing you can do to establish credit is to get an installment loan such as a student loan or a car loan (see Section Four, Chapter One). When considering an auto loan, if the terms you have been offered are not satisfactory, it might be beneficial to have a parent or guardian cosign on the loan in order to possibly get a preferred interest rate. If you are getting an auto loan and a parent or guardian cosigns, then you will want to request that the vehicle be titled in your name only. If you already own a car, then contact a local bank or financial institution and apply for an installment loan (using the auto as collateral if it is not that old and is within the lending institution's guidelines). Borrow the smallest amount possible and repay the loan within six to twelve months, if feasible. **It is important with any type of loan you get that the pay history *will be reported* to one of the three major credit bureau agencies.** It does not do your credit rating any good to get a loan through a local financial institution if that company does not report your payment record to a major credit bureau agency.

If you are making rent payments, whether to a parent, a relative, or a landlord, you need to make sure that you pay the rent with a check or money order and *keep the receipts*. This will help you to establish another credit reference by being able to prove that you have paid your rent on time. You can keep proof of the rent payments with your monthly bank statements, your cancelled checks (if your bank returns them to you), or your money order receipts (if paid by money order). This will also prove to be a good credit reference when you start looking to buy your first house (see Section One).

Once you have established three or four credit references, **it is a good time to just let your credit references mature and for you to develop a good repayment habit.** Over the next twelve months or so, you should concentrate on the consumer loans that you have opened. Do not apply for any more credit. You have enough credit to get started. Use the credit wisely. Buy gas using your gas card. Buy clothes on the department store charge card. Keep the bank statements to your checking account for at least the last twelve-month cycle. **The goal is to establish a good repayment history by paying your bills on time each month and to have this information reported to a major credit bureau agency.** You will probably start to get a flood of credit solicitations in the mail. Do not apply to or answer them. Concentrate on building a good foundation with the credit you have opened. In establishing your credit, financial institutions are not impressed by how many loans or by how much credit you have. Instead, they are interested in the record of how well and how timely you have made your payments to whatever credit you have been granted.

Chapter 2: Cosigning for Credit

When you are asked by someone else to consider cosigning on a loan, there are two questions that will be important for you to ask yourself: (1) If the borrower does not pay this loan, can I afford to pay it? And (2) if the borrower defaults on this loan or damages my credit rating, will I *honestly* be able to remain friendly and cordial to this person? **If you answer *no* to either one of these questions or if you are not**

100% comfortable with the implications, then I would advise you *not* to sign for the loan. I would *not* recommend cosigning for a loan if you are only boyfriend and girlfriend, long time coworkers, or friends. I would recommend cosigning if you are a family member or a "very close" friend of the family, and you both have discussed the situation openly and honestly.

There are two main reasons for a borrower to need a cosigner. The borrower either has no credit or the person has poor credit. If the individual has no credit, then he or she is probably trying to establish credit, but might need some help in qualifying (refer to Chapter One). If this is the case, then the cosigner will most likely be a parent, guardian, sibling, or relative. This is the best situation for which to cosign for a loan. However, before you agree to cosign, you need to have an open and frank conversation with the primary borrower, the person borrowing the money. You need to discuss the importance of paying debts on time, the need to establish a good repayment history, and what consequences will occur if this is not done.

The second situation in which a borrower might need a cosigner is that the individual has poor credit. Have a conversation with this person to find out how he or she arrived at this low credit rating. The low credit rating could be the result of a type of life-changing event such as: A separation or divorce, a major unforeseen medical condition, the death of a spouse or loved one, the loss of a job, or being laid off. If this is the case, and it was *an isolated incident*, I would consider cosigning for this individual. It is still important to make sure that you can answer "yes" to the first two questions listed at the beginning of this chapter. However, I would only agree to cosign *after* the crisis has passed and provided the individual *had* a good credit rating prior to this life-changing event.

If the borrower needs a cosigner because of bad credit due to his or her own financial irresponsibility, this indicates that he or she cannot properly budget money nor live within their means, therefore you should **NOT** cosign. No matter how many excuses or pleases they give you, you should not cosign unless you are prepared to pay for the loan when they fail to make the payments. This is the worst cosigning scenario because this type of individual generally has never paid for credit on time and probably never will.

If you agree to cosign, then there are a couple of steps you need to take to ensure that you are fully aware of the type of loan for which you will be cosigning and what the terms will be. As a potential cosigner, ask the primary borrower to make an appointment for both of you to meet with the lender to discuss the details of the loan. However, due to privacy laws, the lender may not be able to discuss specifics about the other person's credit rating with you present. Also, **as a cosigner, it is YOUR responsibility to make sure that the payments are made on time.**

Once you have cosigned for the loan, do not rely on the primary borrower to tell you that he or she is making the monthly payment. You have more to lose should the primary borrower default on the loan because you are the one with the good credit rating. Make sure that the financial institution documents that, as the cosigner, you want to be called if a loan payment becomes more than fifteen days late. **Take a very proactive approach to monitoring these payments.** Taking these precautions and knowing what you have agreed to do by cosigning will ensure that the relationship between the borrower and you will continue and that the loan will be repaid as agreed, thus preserving your credit and helping to repair or establish theirs!

Chapter 3: Divorcing and How it Affects Your Credit

Going through a divorce is never easy. When a marriage ends, details such as dividing the assets (who gets what) and deciding what the financial arrangements will be (who pays whom) must be attended to. **But, what people fail to realize is that until all joint, cosigned and even authorized user loans are closed or cancelled, the couple will still be linked financially.** Until the closing or cancellation of all joint debts is done, your credit will be affected should the ex-spouse fail to pay his or her part. This is true even if the divorce decree specifically states that the other party is responsible for the house payment, the charge card, the car loan, or whatever. The financial institution or bank that granted a loan to *both* parties does not care what the divorce papers declare. What matters to the collection department of that institution is that it has two individuals who are equally and contractually obligated for the debt because both signatures are present on the promissory note.

In my experiences as a collection manager, whenever this type of situation arose I would always contact whoever had the better credit rating to inform him or her that the joint loan was past due and that it was being reported as such against their credit. If a loan originally granted to the married couple should go into default status (charged-off), both parties can be taken to court in order to collect the debt. Once the court has made its ruling that the defendants (both borrowers) are responsible for paying the debt, it is up to the individual who repaid the loan to sue the nonpaying ex-spouse to collect any damages or costs they incurred with having to pay off the loan that the divorce decree said the other party was supposed to pay.

Fortunately, there are a couple of things you can do to protect yourself and your good credit rating when divorcing. The first thing to do when divorce is imminent is to order a copy of your credit report in order to see exactly what credit is open and jointly held. Next, you should personally contact all credit card companies with which you have any joint and authorized user charge cards to get them closed. Make sure to get confirmation *in writing* from the credit card company that each line has been closed. If you are designated as an authorized user on any charge cards that your ex-spouse plans to keep open, contact those financial institutions and have your name removed. Again, get the response in writing. Additionally, if you are a joint debtor on any installment loans or charge cards, contact the lender and inquire about either getting the loan refinanced or modify the loan terms in order to get the loan put into one name or the other while the credit rating on the loan is still good. This offers some protection if, out of spite, the ex-spouse purposely lets his or her credit go bad, files a bankruptcy, or simply is unable to pay the debt. As long as a debt or loan is still listed as being a joint account, if the ex-spouse should default, the negative rating will be reported to both credit bureaus. **The key is that the sooner you can get financially separated from your ex-spouse the better off you and your credit will be.**

Chapter 4: Overcoming Credit Problems and Re-Establishing Credit

Some people would argue that the hardest thing to do regarding credit is to reestablish your credit rating after it has been badly damaged. **Having good credit takes years to establish and discipline to maintain.** On the other hand, **good credit can be destroyed in a matter of months.** Some credit damages are easier to repair than others. The extent of the credit damage will determine how much of an uphill battle you face. For instance, having a couple of loans that are thirty days late (owing more than one payment) is an easier problem to correct than having a loan on your record that was charged off because of habitual nonpayment. Most everyone will have to deal with economic hardships or money scarcity at times throughout their life. The key is to keep your credit rating as good as possible during the lean times in order to get your financial affairs back in order more quickly.

If you are experiencing a money crunch or a short-term interruption to your income, there are a couple of proactive things that you can do to buy some time and protect your good credit rating. A money crunch or short-term interruption to your income might be due to a seasonal or temporary layoff, changing jobs, the birth of a baby, a major car repair bill, an unforeseen illness, or medical emergency. These short-term interruptions are all characterized as unforeseen events that leave you short on cash with which to pay your monthly bills. The first thing that you should do when you experience this type of situation is to contact the creditors to whom you owe money. Most banks and lenders are very willing to work out a revised payment plan for you when you are honest with them and they understand that this is a *temporary* situation.

During times of financial difficulties there are a few options that may be available for paying installment loans. They include a temporary repayment plan, a deferment, or a permanent modification of the loan terms. Option one is to see if the lending institution would set up a temporary repayment plan for you. This could be arranged so that you would make a partial payment for the first month and then break up the difference of the remaining amount over the next two or three months. As an example, let's say that one of your regular monthly payments is $200.00. On a temporary repayment plan, you would pay $100.00 for the first month. Then for the next two months, you would pay $250.00. That is $200.00 for the regularly scheduled monthly payment and $50.00 for the partial payment. On the fourth month, you would return to paying the regular monthly payment of $200.00.

The second option would be to request a one or two month deferment. A deferment means that you would skip a monthly payment or two and have those payments placed at the end of the loan. Usually there is a small fee for this service and you may have to pay any interest due on the loan.

A third option is to ask the lender if your monthly payments can be permanently lowered by having the loan terms modified. This means that your monthly repayment schedule would be re-amortized and extended by six or twelve months. With any route you choose, **the key is to contact the lender and make payment arrangements *before* your loan becomes delinquent.**

For a revolving type of consumer loan, there are a couple of options as well if you are experiencing a money crunch or a short-term interruption to your income. The main difference with a line of credit or charge card, as compared to an installment loan, is that the interest owed is not predetermined. The interest owed is calculated on a monthly basis by using what your average balance for the previous month was.

Option one would be to request that you only pay the interest payment for the month. In this example, suppose your credit card loan balance is $5,000.00. If the minimum monthly payment is three percent of the loan balance, then the regular payment would be $150.00. If the interest rate was 10%, then the interest due for the month would only be approximately $40.00.

10.00%	Interest Rate		$5,000.00	Loan Balance
÷ 12	Months		X 0.008	Interest Factor
0.008	Interest Factor		$40.00	Interest Payment

Option two would be to ask if your monthly payment could be switched to a fixed payment amount for a couple of months (or permanently). This might require that your revolving line of credit be closed. But this may help you to better budget your monthly expenses and keep your credit rating in good shape, which is more important than having available credit.

Sometimes, overcoming credit problems is the result of having to face a major, traumatic, and life-changing event. These traumatic, life-changing events can take as long as six months to a year or longer before full recovery. A traumatic, life-changing event could be the unexpected death of a spouse, the closing of a plant causing permanent work displacement, a prolonged strike at work, a divorce and custody battle, or a major illness. Most borrowers will probably experience a traumatic, life-changing event at least once in their borrowing money life. If you are not prepared for the unexpected, it could have dire consequences on your credit. It could force you to file for bankruptcy protection, liquidate precious assets, and/or cause your credit score to go into a major tailspin.

It is hard to plan for these events and impossible to predict them, but being financially responsible will make repairing your credit a lot easier. Keeping a good credit score, paying your bills on time, and having a low credit utilization ratio (that is the amount of credit you owe versus how much credit you have available on your revolving charge lines) will all help to show *a pattern* of good credit management. This way when a traumatic, life-changing event has occurred, the lender will be able to determine from your credit file that there was a *specific* period of difficulty that was out of the ordinary and not the norm for you.

There are two things that I would recommend that you do when this happens. The first is to contact the major credit reporting agency that services your geographical area shortly after you have recovered from this life changing event to request a copy of your credit report. If you are not sure which credit reporting company is prevalent in your area, contact the local branch manager with whom you do your banking. (The three main credit-reporting agencies are listed at the end of Section Six, Chapter Four.) After reviewing your credit file and determining that all loans are being reported properly, I would recommend that you place a brief explanation or statement at the bottom of your credit file explaining what happened and the period of time involved. This way, your side of the story will be available to the underwriter as he or she is reviewing your credit report. This is a good tool if you tend to borrow through credit card applications, through the mail, or make loan requests over the internet rather than in person.

The second thing is that when you apply for credit in person, divulge information about your life-changing event during the initial application process. This will prepare the lender and underwriter so that he or she knows what to anticipate when reviewing your credit report. Doing so supplies the lender with answers to match with any possible questions that arise once the credit investigation is initiated. Be prepared in advance to give approximate dates for how long this event affected your credit and be able to briefly explain what happened without going into any great detail.

Lack of financial responsibility and a history of poor loan repayment creates the most difficult credit situation from which to break free. If your credit history reveals random charge-offs, judgments and collections, tax liens, or an overall poor credit repayment history, then you will not be able to use the "crutch" of a traumatic, life-changing event as the cause of your money trouble. Though lenders are willing to help borrowers in times of crisis, there must be evidence of a pattern of good credit repayment history prior to and after the event.

To re-establish credit after a poor history of paying credit late has been established will take work on your part. The first thing you will need to do is to see how bad your credit actually is. You can do this by requesting a copy of your credit report. If you have recently been denied credit, then you will be able to request a free copy of your credit file as long as you request the report within sixty days of being denied credit. If you have not applied for credit in a while, then you can request a copy of your report for a small fee. However, some states have a law that allows you to review your credit file for free at least once a year. Listed at the end of Section Six, Chapter Four, you will find information about how you can order a copy of your credit file. You need to review your credit file and determine where your deficiencies are.

The next thing you need to do is devise a plan by deciding what loans to bring current (up to date) first. The most important type of credit is your mortgage loan because you need a place to live. This should *always* be the first creditor that you pay every month. The next most important type of credit is your secured car loan because you need that vehicle to get to and from work so that you can earn money with which to pay your bills. After those two have been taken care of, begin to make payments on loans that can be brought current most quickly. Lastly, after all consumer loans are brought current, I would concentrate on any remaining debts that were charged-off or any unpaid collections.

As you start your credit rehabilitation, you should call each creditor by phone to discuss how you can make your loan(s) current. If the lender arranges a repayment schedule with you, then it is *extremely* important that you can afford the new monthly payments. It is also essential for you to adhere to the repayment schedule terms exactly as agreed. Some unsecured lenders will be willing to accept a lesser dollar amount of what is actually owed as a settlement for the loan. If this happens, **make sure that you get the agreed repayment terms and settlement offer *in writing* from the creditor before you begin to pay.** As you start to make your loans current, your credit score will begin to improve. The sooner you can bring all your loans and debts current the better because the delinquency does remain in your credit file for at least five to seven years. With time and attention to these details, the bad credit will "age" and your credit score will become higher!

Consumer Credit Counseling

Consumer Credit Counseling Service (CCCS) can be a viable alternative for people who are experiencing financial difficulty and having trouble meeting their monthly debt (loan) obligations. **The purpose of CCCS is to help people to get out of debt and to educate them on how to develop a family budget.** You meet with a local representative who reviews your present financial condition and debts. With your input, the representative develops a workable family budget, and negotiates payments on your behalf to your unsecured creditors (mostly charge cards). In turn, you will pay CCCS a one lump sum payment every month and they distribute the monies to the creditors as negotiated. **In order for this to work and to get out of debt, you <u>must</u> follow the plan, make your payment on time to CCCS, and <u>not</u> open up any new credit until you have completed the program.**

There are a lot of companies that you see advertised on television or in media print who offer credit assistance. Some of these companies will charge large fees for their services or deliver poor customer service with no budget-planning courses. This defeats the purpose of consumer credit counseling. You want all of your money (or most of it) to go towards paying off your debt and a counselor who offers help in designing an appropriate family budget for you. Therefore, it is best to find a *local* non-profit credit agency, one that will work in *your* best interest. To find a local and reputable company, you can check with the Better Business Bureau, the local Chamber of Commerce, or with the local bank branch where you have your deposit (checking or saving account) relationship (also see Section Six, Chapter Four).

Chapter 5: Surviving a Bankruptcy

Given today's financial climate, having a bankruptcy is not the end of the world. Fierce competition among lending institutions has lead to the growth of "sub-prime" lending to people with marginal or high risk credit ratings and/or bankruptcies. Also, having a bankruptcy on your credit record does not have the same social stigma as it did twenty or thirty years ago. However, a major drawback is that most high-risk borrowers and those with a bankruptcy will have to pay more to borrow money in the form of higher interest rates and/or higher fees. Another drawback is that a bankruptcy will most likely stay in your credit file for seven to ten years. Depending on the condition of your credit prior to filing, the cause of the bankruptcy, and how you have re-established credit since the discharge date of the bankruptcy will determine what the recovery period will be until you are considered an "A" credit risk again.

There are mainly two types of situations forcing people to file for bankruptcy. The first type of situation is when a person who has had good credit suffers a major, traumatic, and life-changing event. A traumatic, life-changing event could be the unexpected death of a spouse, the closing of a plant causing permanent work displacement, a prolonged strike at work, a divorce and custody battle, or a major illness without any medical insurance. **Having maintained good credit, having a** reputation for paying your bills on time, and not having a high debt load will make recovering from a bankruptcy less difficult and make it easier to re-establish credit. The reason for this is that a lender will be able to see that the bankruptcy was an isolated incident and that prior to this event, you were able to show sound financial responsibility.

The second type of situation where a bankruptcy is filed is when a person has used a lot of credit, carried high loan and high credit card balances, didn't make prompt or sufficient payments, and eventually got in over their head in debt either from their own poor money management skills or a traumatic, life-changing event. This person, prior to the bankruptcy, might have been paying the bills on time (but only made the minimum required monthly payments) or may have started to show signs of delinquency. People finding themselves is this circumstance may try to claim that a life-changing event, whether a minor or major event, is the reason for their delinquency. However, an experienced lender (or underwriter) will be able to see whether that claim is true or false by looking at how much debt was discharged in the bankruptcy and if there were any signs of credit deterioration or delinquency prior to the claimed life-changing event.

On a personal basis, there are two types of bankruptcies you can file. They are the Chapter Seven Bankruptcy and the Chapter Thirteen Bankruptcy. In a Chapter Seven Bankruptcy, the borrower's assets are liquidated by a court appointed trustee in order to repay all or part of the borrower's debt obligations. If there are no assets, the debts are discharged and the unsecured creditors will receive nothing. Most Chapter Seven Bankruptcies are discharged (released with no obligations or penalty), or completed, within eight to twelve months.

In a Chapter Thirteen Bankruptcy, the borrower agrees to an amended repayment (re-organized) plan, called a Wage Earner Plan, of his or her monthly debt and loan obligations. The debtor files this plan with the bankruptcy court and agrees to pay partial payments of the obligations owed to their creditors. Typically, the secured creditors (such as a car loan or a mortgage loan) will receive their regular monthly payment but the unsecured creditors will receive partial payments, if any at all. The repayment plan is typically set up for three to five years. After that, any remaining unsecured balance is discharged (released with no obligations or penalty) from the debtor.

There are a couple of steps that you can take to help rebuild your credit after you have filed for a bankruptcy. The first thing to do is to request a copy of your credit report to make sure that your credit is being reported accurately. If you filed a Chapter Seven Bankruptcy, order a copy of your credit file about sixty to ninety days after your bankruptcy has been discharged. If you filed a Chapter Thirteen Bankruptcy, order your file about six months after you have started your repayment plan. You need to review your credit report to make sure that each creditor is properly reporting your debts to the credit reporting agencies. Sometimes a creditor will still list your debt as open or as a charged off loan when, in fact, the balance was included in your bankruptcy filing and was discharged, or forgiven. Other times you have reaffirmed the debt and have been paying the payment on time but the lender stopped reporting the debt. Reviewing your credit file for accurate reporting will help your chances of re-establishing your credit a little more quickly.

Re-establishing your credit will take time. You will first need to start with paying the loans that were not discharged in the bankruptcy, but reaffirmed (when you agree to continue making monthly payments on certain loans outside of the bankruptcy plan), on time. It is extremely important that these monthly payments are paid on time because you cannot afford a slight slip up or late payment. After a couple of months have passed, the next step is to obtain a new credit card.

However, the credit card may have to be a secured card, which might require a security deposit. Then slowly, as needed, and in a conservative manner, begin to apply for new credit. There is no standard formula to use on re-establishing credit after a bankruptcy because each situation is different; each with its own set of circumstances and repayment terms. **The key is that your remaining loans and any future loans must be repaid on time without the slightest late payment.**

Section VI
Fraud

Introduction

Establishing and building a good credit rating takes years to achieve, but it can be destroyed in a short time if you become a victim of credit fraud. Credit fraud is an ever-increasing problem and will personally cost you a lot of time and energy to correct. **Credit fraud is a crime and you should not feel embarrassed, ashamed, or responsible if it happens to you.** Therefore, once you become aware that you are a victim of fraud, you must take **<u>immediate action</u>**. The longer you wait to take action, the worse the situation can become. The more time that goes by, the more money (credit) the crook can steal, and the harder it will be for you to prove you were a victim. There are generally two types of credit fraud of which you can become a victim. The first type is what I call "family fraud" and the second (and more serious) type of credit fraud is known as identity theft.

Chapter 1: Family Fraud

Family fraud is the less "severe" type of credit fraud. This type of fraud occurs when someone either steals a revolving charge card from you or opens a loan using your name, data, and social security number. **Primarily, the perpetrator of this type of credit fraud is someone whom the victim knows.** In most cases, the perpetrator is a close relative or someone who has access to your home and/or knowledge of your finances. The perpetrator could be an adult child battling an addiction problem, a granddaughter who cares for an elderly grandparent, a sibling who is in a financial bind, or basically anyone who is desperate enough. The characteristics of family fraud are as follows: It is an isolated incident, generally the perpetrator needs to get themselves out of a bind with just one or two loans, and it is carried out by someone the victim knows. Usually, you will not find out about the fraud early because the perpetrator has probably been able to intercept the monthly statements and delinquent notices. Most likely you will find out about the fraud after it has been going on for some time by receiving a phone call from a collector.

This type of fraud is especially tough and can cause emotional distress for you as the victim. Not only will you feel betrayed, but it will force you to do something that probably won't be easy... file legal charges against the individual who committed the fraud. **Only through filing charges against this person will you be able to prove that the debt in question is not your loan or obligation.** A creditor cannot automatically forgive you of a debt without any legal documented proof that it is not yours. Many people who find themselves victims of family fraud choose only to confront the individual with their knowledge of the fraud and hope that the loan will be repaid in a timely manner or paid in full. Others will choose to become responsible for the debt and hope that it does not happen again.

If you suspect that you have been a victim of family fraud, there are a couple of steps you need to take. The first thing you need to do when you believe you have become a victim of family fraud is to call the creditor on the phone. It is best to talk to the manager or a supervisor at the local branch and tell him or her that you believe you are the victim of fraud. Have the manager check your records for any open accounts or any recent credit inquiries under your social security number and name. If a loan or revolving charge account has been opened without your consent, then you should request to see the signed copies of the retail loan application, the loan contract (promissory note), and any other verification documents that might be in the file. If the fraudulent account is an open line of credit or charge card, immediately close the line of credit and make sure that it is not attached to any of your deposit or saving accounts. Also, be sure to have the manager or supervisor flag or mark your account by noting that there has been some suspected fraudulent activity on your account. Make sure that they know that you want to be contacted by phone if anyone attempts you use your name and/or social security number again.

After you have determined that there has been fraudulent activity against you, the next thing to do is to decide whether or not you are going to notify the authorities and file a criminal police report. This is a difficult decision that you have to make. At this point, you have two choices: **Either you file a criminal police report concerning the fraud or you choose to become responsible for the debt and have it remain a part of your credit file**. You are responsible for the timely repayment of the debt unless you decide to "prove" that it is not your debt by helping the creditor with legal proceedings against the perpetrator. The creditor will not forgive the debt simply because you claim that it is not your loan. If you decide to keep this incident out of the hands of the law, then you will become responsible for the debt and any late payments become part of *your* credit history. You should also contact other close family members to make them aware of the fraud so that they to do not become a target as well.

The third step is to notify the three main credit reporting agencies (listed in Chapter Four) and inform them that you have become a victim of fraud. Have them put a fraud alert in your credit file. That means that you will be personally contacted if any inquiries are made using your social security number and/or name. Whether or not you have chosen to take legal action, you should write a brief statement to be kept at the bottom of your credit file stating that the loan in question is not yours, but was fraudulently opened by a family member. Most lenders will overlook this "bad" credit situation if it is the only blemish in your credit file. Particularly if you make them aware that this was a result of fraud and was *an isolated incident.* Lenders will hold you in good faith if the loan is being repaid, maybe late, but not charged off. Another consequence, if you have decided to accept responsibility for the debt, is that it will become part of your debt-to-income ratio. You could also be declined for future loans based on its credit rating, especially if the loan is charged off (bank terminology meaning uncollectible). If the loan gets charged off due to non-payment, then you will most likely have to pay off or settle the debt before you can be approved to borrow any more money.

If you were fortunate, the individual may have repaid the loan in full and on time, even though the loan was fraudulently acquired. Consider yourself lucky. You will have another good credit reference added to your credit file. As a preventative measure, I would still advise you to notify the credit bureaus as outlined in the third step because the next time you might not be so lucky. As a precaution, have them place a fraud alert in your credit file because the perpetrator could strike again. I would also still notify other family members so they are aware of the fraudulent activity. If you uncover who the perpetrator was, you need to make sure that person is aware that you know it was them and that any future fraudulent activity will cause you to file a police report.

Chapter 2: Identity Theft

The most serious type of credit fraud is called identity theft. **In cases of identity theft, the person steals or acquires your name, your social security number, and can severely damage your good credit.** The difference between family fraud and identity theft is that, in the latter, the person is usually someone whom you do not know or someone with whom you had a brief encounter. This type of person has a criminal mindset and intends to live as long as possible from profits off of your good name and credit. There are numerous ways in which identity theft could occur, through someone stealing your wallet or purse, by breaking into your home, by going through your garbage, or by stealing your mail. Identify thieves are also con artists who take advantage of your honesty and good nature. An unscrupulous individual at any place of business can perpetrate identity theft. **Do not blame yourself if you become a victim of identity theft.** Instead, when it happens, you must take immediate action. The longer you wait, the more damage will be done to your credit, and the harder it will be for you to prove that it was fraud.

If your personal information is stolen, **the first thing that you must do is to file a police report in the jurisdiction where the crime took place.** If you are unsure where the crime occurred, but are certain that your identity was stolen, then contact your local police department and file a report. The key is that you must file the police report as soon as you become aware that your identity or personal belongings were stolen. This helps you and your creditors establish a time line of when you stopped being responsible for any credit *usage*. However, you are still responsible for any outstanding loan balance up to that point, so you should continue to make regular *minimum* monthly payments on the account. If the creditor tells you not to make any payments until it is determined what you are responsible for, then get it *in writing* so that your credit rating will not be impaired.

The next thing that you must do is to place phone calls to each of the financial institutions and banks where you have open revolving lines of credit, credit cards, checking or saving accounts, and any active ATM or debit cards. You need to advise these companies that your identity has been stolen. I would recommend that you close all of your accounts and open up new ones with new account numbers. This way, if and when the thief attempts to use the account, the transaction will not be approved. Hopefully, your closed accounts will be flagged by the financial institution as reported stolen. Many stores, gas stations, and ATM machines are now equipped with surveillance cameras. If the card has been flagged as stolen and the thief attempts to use it, then he or she might be caught in act.

The third thing you must do is to alert all three major credit bureau agencies, listed at the end of this section in Chapter Four, and notify them that your identity has been stolen. An "alert" will be placed in your credit file. This way, if the criminal possessing your stolen information attempts to obtain a new charge card or apply for credit using your name, a "red" flag will come up when the credit report is ordered. This will block the transaction from being approved. Hopefully, an alert sales clerk or manager will be able to recognize the fraud during the transaction and contact the local authorities to report the incident so that the criminal will be caught red handed! Lastly, you may want to contact the Social Security Administration to notify them that your social security number has been stolen.

The last thing to do is to request a copy of your credit file, preferably the main credit bureau agency who services the geographical area where you live, approximately sixty to ninety days after you have notified the credit bureaus of the identify theft. If you do not know which credit reporting company that is, then you can ask your local bank branch manager. Review your credit file to verify that all credit account balances are correct and that all open and active loans are, in fact, yours. Notice whether or not any fraudulent activity has been flagged or removed from your credit report. This way, the next time you apply for credit there shouldn't be any surprises.

Identity Theft is not a victimless crime. It is a very serious situation. You need to remember to follow your "gut" instincts. If you feel that your name and good credit have been victimized, then you need to take immediate steps to notify your creditors and the authorities. Credit fraud is a crime, so you should not feel embarrassed or ashamed if it happens to you. Remember, establishing and building a good credit rating takes years to achieve, but it only takes a short time to destroy.

Chapter 3: Preventative Measures

Now that you are aware of the two types of credit fraud; family fraud and the more serious identity theft, we need to examine some ways to reduce your risk of becoming a victim. Most of these techniques are simple to do and cost little to implement. Some are as simple as changing your behavior. We live in such a mobile and fast paced environment that obtaining credit is much easier. It is up to you to be prudent and cautious to help prevent your financial information from getting into the wrong hands.

- **Pay close attention to your incoming monthly bills.** Report any discrepancies to that place of business immediately. Review the charges on the monthly statement to make sure that they are indeed your purchases. Keep at least the last 12 months worth of bills and monthly statements in a safe and secured place.

- Order a copy of your credit report at least once a year to verify that all information listed is correct and accurate. You also want to verify that all debts or loans listed in your file are indeed yours.

- Have only your first initial or short name (instead of your proper first name) and your last name printed on your checks. Do not include your middle name or initial. This way if someone steals your checks they will not know how you sign your name.

- **Do not put your social security number on your checks.** Your social security number is your most important form of personal identification and it needs to be protected. You do not know who has access to the information on the checks as it clears its way through the system.

- List only your address, city and state on your checks, **not** your home phone number. If you have a post office box, use that instead of your physical home address.

- Some states print social security numbers as your identification numbers on driver's licenses. Request that your social security number be removed and get a generic identification number. If at all possible, do **not** carrying anything that has your social security number in your wallet or purse.

- Make a list of all the creditors with which you have open loans, credit cards, revolving lines of credit, checking accounts, and deposit accounts and keep the list in a secure location such as a fire proof safe or safety deposit box. You should have the company names and toll-free numbers easily accessible.

- **Invest in a paper shredder for the home.** Shredders can be purchased for under $25.00. Shred all documents that have (pertinent) financial or personal information on them. This includes documents such as bank statements, monthly credit card statements, utility bills, insurance bills, etc. Basically, you want to shred any document that shows your address, social security number, or an account number. Shred any pre-approved credit card solicitation offers that bear a confirmation number, any balance transfer checks, and blank checks that credit card companies now mail.

- **Never** give out your social security number and/or your mother's maiden name to any online solicitations or to a telemarketer unless you are one hundred percent certain it is a legitimate business. Particularly, beware of solicitors who *contact you* rather than you contacting them. You can request that they mail you a brochure, advertisement, or literature about the product or service that they were trying to solicit so that you can determine the legitimacy of the offer and then respond.

- Do **not** mail anything that you would not want to end up in the wrong hands from the mailbox in front of your house where it would remain unguarded all day. Anyone driving by, who spots the red flag up, can easily steal the envelopes from the mailbox. This would give the thief the perfect opportunity to copy, alter, or cash checks. Mail any checks, monthly bills, loan applications, etc., from your local post office, a U.S. Mailbox, or from work.

- If you are completing an online loan application that was **sent to you**, you should check to make sure that it is a legitimate business by typing in the company's web address (the address where the email originated from) *by hand* to your web browser. (Do not click on the "submit" button at the beginning or end of the application.) Many scam emails try to confuse people by hiding their fraudulent web address behind an apparently safe looking label similar to a trusted company's or with an address that is a couple of letters different that the real web address.

If you have any other suggestions or ideas about how to safeguard your identity and/or protect others from becoming victims of fraud, please visit our website at www.theborrowingmoneyguide.com and have your suggestion added. Please visit our website regularly for the up to the minute tips and suggestions for safeguarding identity and credit.

Chapter 4: Important Phone Numbers and Addresses

The three main credit bureaus agencies are:

- Equifax - www.equifax.com

> To report fraud: 1-800-525-6285 or 888-766-0008
> To request a copy of your credit report: 1-800-685-1111
>
> Mailing address: P.O. Box 740241
> Atlanta, GA. 30374

- Experian - www.experian.com   (formerly known as TRW)

> To report fraud: 1-888-397-3742 or 800-311-4769
> To request a copy of your credit report: 1-888-397-3742
>
> Mailing address: P.O. Box 2104
> Allen, TX. 75013-2104

- Trans Union - www.transunion.com

> To report fraud: 1-800-680-7289
> To request a copy of your credit report: 1-800-888-4213
>
> Mailing address: P.O. Box 2000
> Chester, PA. 19022

- To "opt out" of the three major credit reporting agencies solicitation mailing lists call: 1-888-5OPT OUT or 1-888-567-8688.

To check your credit score:

- FICO – www.myfico.com   (Fair, Isaac & Company, which is the most widely used scoring model)

Phone number: 800-726-1421

Mailing address: 3B Customer Service
P.O. Box 222455
Chantilly, VA. 20153-2455

If you are a victim of credit fraud or identity theft contact:

- Federal Trade Commission - www.ftc.gov

  Phone number: 1-877-IDTHEFT (1-877-438-4338)

  FTC Consumer Identity Theft website:
  www.comsumer.gov/idtheft

- Social Security Administration - www.ssa.gov

  SSA fraud hotline: 1-800-269-0271

- National Fraud Information Center - www.fraud.org

  Phone number: 1-800-876-7060

To be removed from telemarketing or solicitation lists contact:

- The National Do Not Call Registry - www.donotcall.gov

  Phone number: 1-888-382-1222

- Direct Marketing Associations - www.the-dma.org

  Mailing address: DMA-*Mail* Preference Services
  Attn: Dept 10106565
  P.O. Box 282
  Carmel, N.Y. 10512

  Mailing address: DMA-*Telephone* Preference Services
  Attn: Dept. 10106524
  P.O. Box 282
  Carmel, N.Y. 10512

To get counseling for your credit contact:

- National Foundation for Credit Counseling (NFCC) - www.debtadvice.org

  Phone number: 301-589-5600
  To find a local member agency: 800-388-2227

  Mailing address: 801 Roeder Rd.
  Suite 900
  Silver Spring, MD. 20910

Miscellaneous Information:

- The Better Business Bureau Online - www.bbbonline.org

- U.S. Government Hoax Busters - www.hoaxbusters.ciac.org
  (comprehensive list of scams and frauds)

Section VII
Glossary

Affiliated Business Arrangement: an early disclosure form that discloses any business relationship the lender may have with other companies that are providing services necessary to complete the mortgage loan transaction. The lender may receive a financial benefit from the fee collected by the affiliated company because the affiliated company is a wholly owned subsidiary of the lender. This form is part of the Pre-disclosure Package.

Amortization: the repayment of a debt or loan by periodic, usually monthly, payments of principle and interest resulting in a declining principle balance and eventual repayment of the debt or loan in full.

Amortization Table: a table commonly used in mortgages and installment loans showing the number of payments due, the amount of each scheduled installment payment, the interest and principle amount due for each scheduled payment, the declining principle balance, and number of months or years needed to fully repay the debt.

Appraisal: the market value of your home as compared to recent sales of similar houses in your immediate neighborhood or geographical area.

ARM Loan (Adjustable Rate Mortgage): a mortgage loan that has a fixed interest rate and monthly payment for only a short period of time, usually three to five years, then gets converted to a variable interest rate loan for which the interest rate will begin to adjust and change.

Balloon Loan: a loan that has a fixed interest rate and a fixed monthly payment for a period of time that is usually five to fifteen years, but the monthly payment is amortized over, or based on, a longer period of time, usually for thirty years. When the loan matures, there is a balance remaining that needs to be paid off or refinanced into another loan.

Bankruptcy: legal proceedings for adjusting the debts owed by an individual or business because they are unable to meet the contractual obligations to all their creditors. The debtor's finances are placed under the control of a Bankruptcy

Trustee who manages the debtor's affairs for the benefit of the creditors. For consumers, the two types of bankruptcy filings are Chapter 7 and Chapter 13. (See Chapter 7 Bankruptcy and Chapter 13 Bankruptcy)

Borrower: a person who obtains funds or money from another source, typically called a lender, and repays the debt in future interest and principle payments by signing a promissory note with the lender.

Break-even Point: is the point at which the monthly savings between the old and new monthly mortgage payment *equals* the closing cost of the new mortgage loan.

Bridge Loan: a short-term consumer loan, typically six or twelve months, where the borrower cashes out the equity in the house that he or she has for sale to cover the closing cost and/or down payment associated with a house that he or she will purchase before the other residence is sold.

Cash Option: a sales promotion, offered by a business, which helps it to sell large ticket merchandise or service contracts. Customers are given a certain amount of time (usually ninety-days, six months, or twelve months) to pay off the loan interest free.

Chapter 7 Bankruptcy: the debtor's (borrower's) assets are liquidated by a court appointed trustee in order to repay all or part of the borrower's debt obligations to his or her creditors. If there are no assets, the debts are discharged (released with no obligations or penalty) and the unsecured creditors will receive nothing.

Chapter 13 Bankruptcy: the debtor (borrower) agrees to an amended repayment (re-organized) plan, called a Wage Earner Plan, of his or her monthly debt obligations. The debtor must file a repayment budget plan with the bankruptcy court and agree to pay partial payments of the obligations owed to his or her creditors. Typically, the secured creditors (such as a car loan or a mortgage loan) will receive their regular monthly payment but the unsecured creditors will receive partial payments. The repayment plan is typically setup for three or five years and, after that, any remaining unsecured balance is discharged (released with no obligations or penalty) from the debtor.

Co-Borrower: a person who signs a promissory note as the second borrower. This act gives the loan additional security or adds credit quality to the loan to overcome a primary borrower's credit deficiencies. The co-borrower is also contractually obligated to pay the monthly loan payment. Also known as a co-maker or a cosigner.

Co-Maker: See Co-borrower

Conventional Mortgage Loan: a fixed or adjustable rate first mortgage loan that meets certain underwriting standards in order to be sold on the secondary mortgage market. The main purchaser of conventional mortgage loans on the secondary market is Freddie Mac or Fannie Mae.

Cosigner: See Co-Borrower

Credit Bureau: an agency that gathers data for credit grantors on consumer's credit repayment histories and debt obligations. The three main credit bureau agencies are: Experian, Equifax, and TransUnion.

Credit Fraud: when a person intentionally steals your name, social security number, and/or account information for their own personal gain causing injury to the credit file of the victim. Two main types of credit fraud are: Family Fraud and Identity Theft.

Credit Insurance: insurance purchased by the borrower to protect the loan against any abnormal or unforeseen event. There are four main types of credit insurance products: Credit life, credit disability or accident and health, involuntary unemployment insurance, personal property insurance.

Credit Report: a report that details the repayment histories and debt obligations of an individual for credit grantors such as banks, credit unions, and finance companies.

Credit Score: an internal scoring model or grading tool that is widely used by most lenders to determine the risk grade of an applicant and the probability (or likelihood) that the loan will default. The higher the credit score, the less likely a loan will default. Some of the common factors that influence the credit score are: Previous credit history, income, assets, length of employment, and a previous bankruptcy.

Debt-to-Income Ratio: a ratio of your total monthly debts excluding utility bills, but including your monthly mortgage payment, divided by your gross monthly income.

Deed of Trust: a notarized legal document that is recorded in the land records room at the local courthouse in the jurisdiction where the real estate collateral being used for the loan is located in order to place a lien against the property by the note holder.

Delinquent Account (loan): the repaying of a contractual obligation late or after its due date. In most cases, a loan or debt is considered late if the monthly payment is more than thirty days past due from the current payment due date.

Demand Note: a short-term consumer loan, usually for ninety days or six months, with no scheduled monthly payments in-between, for the purpose of using cash now and repaying the debt with interest in full with a lump sum cash repayment at loan maturity.

Discount Rate: the interest rate the Federal Reserve charges banks for overnight funds (money) or short-term loans.

Early Disclosures: see Pre-disclosure Real Estate Package.

Early Truth in Lending: an early disclosure form that lists the interest rate, annual percentage rate, and monthly principle and interest payment associated with your mortgage loan. It is part of the Pre-disclosure Package. Information in this form is used by borrowers to compare different mortgage loan offers.

Easement: a right of way for a person or company (such as a utility company) to use part of your land for their benefit.

Escrow: an agreement authorizing the holding of funds by a bank to pay real estate taxes, homeowner's insurance and private mortgage insurance on behalf of a borrower for the property held as collateral by a mortgage loan.

Family Fraud: an isolated incident where an individual known to the victim steals a revolving charge card or opens a loan under the victim's name and social security number. (See also Credit Fraud and Identity Theft)

Federal Reserve: a federal agency created by the federal government to control the money supply for the United States in order to attempt to keep the economy growing and inflation under control.

First Mortgage: Any type of mortgage loan when the deed of trust is placed in first lien position against any real estate property.

Flood Search: a federal requirement to determine if your house is physically located in an area that is prone to flooding. If the structure is located in a flood plain, then you will be required to obtain a separate flood insurance policy.

Fraud: as it is related to credit, see Credit Fraud.

Good Faith Estimate: an early disclosure form that lists all the estimated closing costs associated with your mortgage loan. It is part of the Pre-disclosure Package. Information in this form is used to compare different mortgage loan offers.

Gross Monthly Income: the earned income listed on your paycheck before any taxes, insurance, retirement or other deductions are subtracted out.

Guarantor: a person who signs the promissory note (loan contract) guaranteeing to pay off the debt and assume the liability of the debt should the primary borrower default on the debt, but is *not* responsible for paying the monthly payments.

HELOC (Home Equity Line of Credit): see Line of Credit Loan.

Home Equity Loan: see Second Mortgage.

Home Inspection: a visual inspection performed on the house you are buying to detect any defects in the house.

Homeowner's Insurance: it protects your home in the event that it is destroyed or damaged. The insurance policy should come with a "replacement" cost stipulation that your home will be repaired or replaced at today's costs. Flood damage is generally not covered.

Identity Theft: when a person unknown to the victim intentionally and illegally uses (steals) the name, social security number, and credit of the victim for their own personal gain. This is the more serious form of credit fraud. (See also Credit Fraud and Family Fraud)

Installment Loan: a contractual obligation where the borrower agrees to repay a debt (or loan) in the form of regular monthly payments of principle and interest to the lender until the debt (or loan) has been repaid in full.

Jumbo Mortgage Loan: a conventional mortgage loan that exceeds the maximum amount the secondary market will buy, such as loans purchased by Freddie Mac or Fannie Mae, and therefore carry a slightly higher interest rate. The current loan limit is $322,700.00.

LIBOR (London Inter-Bank Offered Rate): the key interest rate that the five major banks in London charge each other, other financial institutions, or their most credit worthy large commercial or industrial customers for short term loans or commercial notes.

Lien: when the lender takes a security interest in real property (such as real estate, car title, certificate of deposit, or a savings account to name a few) that is owned by the borrower. This gives the lender the legal right to take (repossess) or sell such property if the corresponding debt (loan) is not repaid on time, as contractually agreed to.

Line of Credit Loan: an open commitment made by a bank or financial institution to borrow money in the future up to a predetermined (credit) limit. The borrower does not have to reapply each time he or she needs money. Funds are accessed at will and are available up to the credit limit.

Loan-to-Value Ratio: the principle balance of a loan(s) that is a lien against the collateral divided by appraised value of the collateral.

Mortgage Broker: an independent third party who brings together the borrower and lender earning a finder's fee (commission) for this service.

Mortgage Insurance: default insurance required on conventional first mortgage loans when you finance more than eighty percent of the appraised value of the home in one loan.

Mortgage Poor: a term signifying the feeling a couple or individual might feel after they have paid their mortgage payment, all creditors, and utility bills for the month and feel that they have no money remaining to enjoy their house or a family life. It means that they purchased a house that was too large for their family budget.

Mortgage Servicing Disclosure: an early disclosure form that indicates what the probability is that your mortgage loan and its servicing rights will be sold to another mortgage lender after the loan has been closed and what your rights are if this happens. This form is part of the Pre-disclosure Package.

Negative Amortization Loan: a loan where the principle balance increases over time because the borrower is allowed to repay a lesser monthly payment than what the fully amortized principle and interest payment is. The difference is added back to the loan balance.

Notice of Right to Cancel: a notice that is given to the borrower at loan closing that gives the borrower the right to cancel the loan transaction within three business days, called the rescission period, at no cost. (See also Rescission Period)

Origination Fee: a fee charged to the borrower by the lender for originating and processing a mortgage loan. One origination fee is equal to 1% of the principle balance of the mortgage loan. The fee must be initially disclosed on the Good Faith Estimate.

Payment Protection: see Credit Insurance.

PMI (Private Mortgage Insurance): see Mortgage Insurance.

Pre-disclosure Real Estate Package: a set of disclosure forms given by the lender to the mortgage applicant at time of application, or mailed within three business days after that, which discloses the borrowers rights, the lenders obligations, and the costs associated with the mortgage loan. Information in this package is used to compare different mortgage loan offers. Some of the forms included are: Good Faith Estimate, Early Truth In Lending, Affiliated Business Arrangement, and Mortgage Servicing Disclosure.

Prepaid Point: see Origination Fee.

Prepayment Penalty: a fee paid to the lender for the privilege of paying off a loan prior to maturity to compensate the lender for the loss of future income on the loan. Most prepayment penalties are for three or five years and are now illegal in some states.

Prime Rate: is the interest rate that large banks charge other financial institutions or their most credit worthy large commercial or industrial customers for short term commercial notes. The Prime rate is based on the Federal Reserve Discount rate, which is controlled by the Federal Reserve Bank.

Promissory Note: A written legal note or promise to pay that serves as evidence of a debt between a borrower and a lender.

Real Estate Taxes: property taxes owed to the city or county based on the value of the collateral owned.

Rescission Period: a federal requirement giving a borrower three business days to cancel a mortgage transaction at no cost to the borrower on certain loan transactions that are secured to the borrower's primary residence.

RESPA (Real Estate Settlement Procedure Act): a federal law requiring lenders to give home mortgage applicants an estimate of the total finance charge and closing costs of the loan prior to closing the loan. Typically the disclosures need to be given to or mailed to the customer within three business days of applying, if the loan is not denied. (See also Pre-disclosure Real Estate Package)

Reverse Mortgage: a mortgage loan in which the borrower typically receives money in monthly installments to supplement his or her monthly income.

Rule of 78's: a method (also know as the Sum of the Digits) used to calculate interest owed when a loan is paid off early. The interest is pre-computed and, unlike simple interest, the majority of interest is paid within the first third of the loan.

Second Mortgage: any type of mortgage loan when the deed of trust is placed in second lien position, behind a first mortgage, against any real estate property.

Settlement Statement: a form given at a mortgage loan closing that lists the exact closing costs associated with the mortgage loan transaction and is signed as part of the loan closing package.

Simple interest: the most popular method used to calculate interest for consumer and mortgage loans where in the interest is computed on the actual principle loan balance without compounding.

Survey: a report that identifies the property lines and any right of ways or easements associate with the land you are buying as being part of the property.

Termite Inspection: an inspection by a licensed exterminator to search for any wood destroying insects or damaged wood from mold or mildew.

Title Search: a search of the land records at the courthouse in the county or city where the collateral property is located to determine who the rightful owner of the property is and if there are any liens or encumbrances against the property.

Traumatic, Life-Changing Event: an unexpected event such as having a spouse pass away, being laid off or permanently displaced at work, a divorce and custody battle, or a major illness that can take six months to a year from which to fully recover financially.

References:
Baron's Business Guide, Dictionary of Banking Terms, 4th edition, , By Thomas P. Fitch, copyright 2000, Baron's Education Series, Inc. 250 Wireless Blvd, Hauppauge, NY, 11788.

Index

Ask the Expert!

Do you have a question for the author?

You may submit a question to be answered by the author. To do so, please visit our website shown under "Contact Us" below. These questions and their answers may be shared publicly on our website for learning purposes. If you would also like an individual response, please provide your email or mailing address.

Share a Success Story?

Would you like to share a success story based on something you learned from the book?

Do you have a success story you would like to share about how "The Borrowing Money Guide©" helped you to successfully borrow money? If you do, you may submit a story that details your successful credit experience. To submit a success story, please see "Contact Us" below.

Comments about the Book?

Is there a comment about the book that you would like to make?

Please visit our website listed below to submit any comments that you have about the book or you may write us at the address listed below.

Want to Contact us?

Web address is: www.theborrowingmoneyguide.com
Mailing address is: JLM Publishing
                    P.O. Box 445
                    Washington, N.J. 07882

Author's email address is: webmaster@theborrowingmoneyguide.com

The
Borrowing Money
Guide©

A "How-To" Book for Consumers

To order additional books:

Visit our website: **www.theborrowingmoneyguide.com**

OR

Send a check or money order for **$14.95** ($12.95 + $2.00 for shipping and handling)

payable to **JLM Publishing** and mail it to: JLM Publishing
P.O. Box 445
Washington, N.J. 07882

- Please allow four to six weeks for delivery.
- Price includes all applicable sales tax.